Small Town Minnesota
A to Z

Small Town Minnesota
A to Z

TONY ANDERSEN

Foreword by Bill Holm

AFTON HISTORICAL SOCIETY PRESS
AFTON, MN

For my mother and father, who gave me the inspiration and encouragement to chase a dream . . .

Edited by Sarah P. Rubinstein

Library of Congress Cataloging-in-Publication Data

Andersen, Tony, 1962–
   Small town Minnesota, A to Z / Tony Andersen; foreword by Bill Holm.--1st ed.
     p. cm.
   ISBN 1-890434-25-6
   1. Minnesota--Pictorial works. 2. Minnesota--Description and travel. 3. Minnesota--History, Local. 4. Cities and towns--Minnesota. 5. City and town life--Minnesota. I. Title

F607.A53 2000
977.6--dc21   00-022487

Printed in Canada

"Love Poem" by Robert Bly in Bill Holm's Foreword is reprinted from *Silence in the Snowy Fields*, Wesleyan University Press, Middletown, CT, 1962. Copyright 1962 Robert Bly. Reprinted with his permission.

The Afton Historical Society Press is a non-profit organization that takes great pride and pleasure in publishing exceptional books on regional subjects.

W. Duncan MacMillan
President

Patricia Condon Johnston
Publisher

Afton Historical Society Press
P.O. Box 100
Afton, MN 55001

Tel: 800-436-8443
email: aftonpress@aftonpress.com
www.aftonpress.com

Contents

Foreword   8

Introduction   13

Foreword

THE SMALL TOWN has had a bad time of it in American literature, as in American life. Think of the list: *Mainstreet*, *Winesburg, Ohio*, *Spoon River*, and on — and on. Think of Mencken's contempt for "The Sahara of Bozart," Scott Fitzgerald's withering disdain for "the lost Swede towns." The fantasy and wish-fulfillment corner of the American imagination has always been in love with the idea of its own emptiness — nature uncorrupted by human beings, the trackless wilderness where, misunderstanding Thoreau, we imagine "the preservation of the world" lies. We romanticize big cities too because money gravitates to them, our achievement of salvation made visible in high buildings, ostentatious mansions, limousines, luxury goods in lit-up windows, fashionable and sophisticated citizens chatting over lobsters and chardonnay — all this garnished with a spicy bouquet of imminent evil: the burglars, killers, junkies, unwashed poor whose presence causes us to tingle at the thought of our own success and good luck. Thus, as our population grows and our large cities metastasize into the countryside, sucking up the rural young who have given up hope for lives or jobs outside of whatever beltway beckons them, we simultaneously try to seal off our parks and preserves from any population other than earnest young backpackers and bad-tempered bears.

Meanwhile, in the presence of this national psychic schizophrenia, life stumbles on in these un-romantic, un-politically correct and most decidedly un-rich, unfashionable small towns that Tony Andersen has chosen to photograph in this lovely book. Trust me, since I live in such a place, and trust the accuracy of Tony Andersen's eye: you do not want to live in these places. Aren't they full of tedious, boring people, mostly old, many overweight, not many "educated" or sophisticated, not many great beauties or "hard bodies," except for the muscles grown from long manual labor, muscles now full of aches, creaks, and arthritis? These people are not dressed by Dayton's or Abercrombie and Fitch or Banana Republic. They wear real overalls, work khakis, housedresses, polyester slacks. Their seed corn hat brims point forward to keep the sun and dust out of the eyes. They wear rubbers in the wintertime to save their good shoes and keep mud off the kitchen floor. They eat mostly hot dish, pot roast, iceberg lettuce, lemon bars, rhubarb pie, and bacon and eggs. They are not troubled by the great inflation in the price of aged balsamic vinegar, and pita bread does not move well at the local bakery. Many of them miss Lawrence Welk.

They think hip-hop is a child's jumping game played with a rope, or heavy metal is what you save behind the grove until the scrap dealer offers you a fair price for it. Most of them faithfully attend Lutheran or Catholic churches (sometimes unexpectedly lovely gems of architecture), more from family habit than religious enthusiasm; the old Lutherans miss the red hymnal, and the old Catholics get nostalgic at the memory of Latin mass. More of them subscribe to the large print edition of *Reader's Digest* than to *Vanity Fair*, *Rolling Stone*, or *Talk*. The landscape outside their towns is mostly flat fields of corn, beans, beets, sunflowers, or cutover scrub pine. Tourists do not come visit them in great numbers: nothing to see, nothing to do, no fun.

But Tony Andersen found something to look at here, and he photographed it with great affection and understanding that grew steadily as he traveled from town to town with his camera. He's a city man and remarks in his Introduction that the behavior of the citizens of these towns surprised him. He expected suspicion, maybe even a ferocious dog or two, but instead got dinner, stories, curiosity, gallons of coffee, and yards of bars — not so much the clichéd "Minnesota nice," but Minnesota civil, decent, courteous, neighborly, as if all human beings, even if they don't look alike or know each other's names, are planetary neighbors and ought to practice good manners toward one another.

He arbitrarily selected his alphabet of towns, requiring only some geographical diversity — Minnesota is a big place, after all — and populations under one thousand. He obviously had no trouble finding places small enough; many towns are under five hundred, the most populous something under eight hundred. These are the towns too small for WalMart or McDonald's or Target, too small in many cases to have hung on to their public schools, most now merged together with ugly acronyms in our recent flurry of hysterical consolidating. Most of these towns are full of dead business buildings, the ghosts of hardware stores, groceries, cafes, garages, implement dealers, and clothiers, the trade having disappeared to strip malls and discounters in bigger towns thirty or forty miles away. Drive a little, save a lot, and kill your main street dead. Modern corporate marketing has not been kind to small places.

It is easy with a camera to make fun of these economically moribund towns with their boarded stores, their mostly elderly citizens. Potbellies, bad dentures, work clothes, and wrinkles can all be used to create a gallery of grotesques — think of Diane Arbus's or Richard Avedon's pictures of the small town West. These are both technically fine photographers, but they do not love what they photograph. Tony Andersen, on the contrary, fell in love with his subjects. I suspect several old ladies almost adopted him, and the old men gave him fatherly instructions on how to roll dice for coffee. His photographs are often full of humor and gaiety, but never of satire or lampoon. Maybe he fell in love, too, with the whole idea of smallness — that human beings can grow souls perfectly well without the benefit either of urban sophistication or of uninhabited wilderness grandeur. Rolf Jacobsen, a lifelong small-town journalist north of Oslo, and one of Norway's greatest twentieth-century poets, has a poem that echoed in my brain when I looked at Tony Andersen's photographic alphabet of small towns.

To Grow Downward

The bigger the cities grow
the smaller the people become.
The higher the houses thrust toward the clouds
the lower those who must live there become.
In New York you are only 10 cm.
In London and Singapore maybe an English foot.
And the cities grow and grow
and your life gets to be worth less and less.
Soon we are only as tall as grass-tufts'
to be cut with a lawnmower
early one Sunday morning.
Or what do you think?

Trans. by Olaf Grinde
from *Breathing Exercises*
White Pine Press 1985

The question at the end of Jacobsen's poem shows typical Norwegian modesty — a quality not unknown among the descendants of Norwegian immigrants in Minnesota. "What do you think?" Are the citizens of Argyle or Odessa or Zumbro Falls bigger (in an interior sense) than their counterparts in Edina or Fridley or St. Paul or Maplewood?

What is "big" in these towns? The signs that announce them for one thing; how many huge decorated signs greet drivers at the city limits to tell them they've arrived at Jasper, for example. "If you lived here, you'd be home now" many of them say. You might be one of three hundred, and your neighbors would have missed you, have spotted you driving into town, and wait to interrogate you for news of your travels. "How are things up in the Cities, then? Did you get caught in that big traffic?" Here in Halstad, or Miltona, or Taunton, you have a name and are addressed by it — always. Your neighbors know your father's name too, and your grandmother's maiden name. Here you cannot escape connection, but that may be only another word for civilization.

Much of the public life in small towns goes on in cafes, where locals exchange news and stories, play cards, shake dice, drink gallons of thin, watery coffee — if it's weak, you can drink more; no market for Starbucks' double espresso here. If you know what's good for you, eat the "special," maybe a beef commercial with some canned green beans and a bowl of slaw on the side. Cafes — and taverns — are always the last businesses to close in dying towns. Humans want a forum for public talk, and they will, by God, have one close at hand, even if they have to drive to St. Cloud for groceries afterwards. I live next to

Taunton and loved Tony Andersen's photograph of four not quite young gentlemen having a jaw over coffee at Rusty's Corner Cafe. "There's Franz Breyfogle," I said to whoever was present. "He started the cafe years ago, then sold it to his niece and her husband. If Franz is feeling ambitious, he makes homemade horseradish for the hamburgers. Best hash browns in the state. I wonder how his garden is doing this year." That's the "small" mind talking, but even if you don't know Franz, you can intuit the lives at that cafe table from Tony Andersen's photograph. We all know somebody, or at least we're supposed to in a sane world.

Reading the names of these towns makes a choral song of our history — the ghosts of Indian tribes, immigrants, grand and famous names, sometimes the pure whimsy of namers: Gonvick, Storden, Upsala, Odessa, Yucatan, or Kelliher, Nicollet, Roosevelt, and my favorite, Donnelly (after old Ignatius, one of Minnesota's great eccentrics). Isle, on the shore of Mille Lacs, pronounced Milax in Minnesota French, provides a fine example of one of my favorite small-town phenomena, the enormous statues of whatever the town is famous for; in this case the world's largest concrete walleye pike.

Tony Andersen climbed a lot of water towers to get photographs with a sense of size and magnitude in these small places. From this height — unrivaled in most towns except for the grain elevator — you can survey the curve of the earth, savor its roundness. It is possible to fall off the edge of a flat world — but if every small place is part of a circle, then it leads to other places, and even, if you travel far enough, back home to itself. Columbus didn't need the *Nina* and the *Pinta* and the *Santa Maria* to prove the earth round. He could have simply climbed a water tower and looked at the horizon.

Cameras can't do everything; they cannot photograph the two greatest gifts of life in a small place far from a big place: silence and darkness. An old college friend of mine made an early fortune in stocks so he bought himself what only the rich can afford in cities — privacy. I went to see his new house in the suburbs of Minneapolis, a mammoth mansion tucked away in deep woods on a lake, perhaps a million dollars' worth of real estate. I stepped out from his vast living room one night to look and listen. At the bottom of what ought to have been silence, Interstate 394 hummed steadily, a throbbing ground bass. "Does it ever stop?" "Only in blizzards, but after awhile you don't hear it at all." Indeed. I looked up — a few pale stars, but most of them faded or gone in the electric pink glow that bathed seven counties. "Ever see northern lights or the Milky Way?" "Have to drive to the lake a hundred miles north. Too bright here." For a million, my old friend buys no stars, no silence. For a few thousand, in most of the places Tony Andersen photographs, you can buy an old house on the edge of town, and after the last pickup has roared off from the liquor store, feast on whole nights full of darkness, so quiet you can hear the blood pulsing through your own arteries. Unlike your wilderness camping expedition, you have the comfort of knowing that a few hundred fellow humans who know your name snore peacefully in their beds nearby, their screen doors and windows open all night, the keys napping in the car's ignition where they belong. Security alarms and motion detectors don't sell well in Taunton or Odessa or Gonvick. The inhabitants still mostly assume that they can sleep in silence and dark protected by the interior presence of civilization among their neighbors.

The town of Cosmos, a stop sign on Highway 7, almost at the belly button of Minnesota, provides the best metaphor to use in looking at Tony Andersen's photographs. The ridiculous name — a ghost of nineteenth-century verbal overkill — inspired the town to its new space-age names like Milky Way Street and Starlite Library. It is the sort of town intelligent children dream of escaping. It is a thousand other towns, like mine, with different names. Could a human being love this place? Could poetry be written there — or great symphonies composed?

When I was a boy, wild to escape my own small town, I went to visit Robert Bly who lived thirty miles away in yet another town that was only slightly too large for this book. One of his early poems I admired goes this way:

Love Poem

When we are in love, we love the grass,
And the barns, and the light poles,
And the small mainstreets abandoned all night.

I asked him what inspired it. He said he was driving home late one summer night from Minneapolis on Highway 7, a curveless belt of concrete that crosses Minnesota all the way to the South Dakota border. He stopped at the stop sign in Cosmos. It's the only stop sign for a hundred miles between Hutchinson and the turnoff to Madison. Not a soul was awake in Cosmos. Main Street hadn't yet graduated to Milky Way. Cosmos, he thought, what a ridiculous name! But even here, there is something to love if we start with love inside us, and so arrived the poem.

Tony Andersen arrived in this alphabet of towns armed not only with his camera, but with love, curiosity, humor, and a good eye. I commend his vision to you.

Bill Holm

Introduction

THE IDEA FOR THIS BOOK first occurred to me some twenty years ago while I was riding in the cramped back seat of the family gas miser (economy is one of Dad's virtues). Having mastered the wonderfully simple workings of my first camera, I fancied myself a photographer and soon developed a heightened interest in traveling. Inspired by Dad's slide shows, I too desired to document the world — or at least the considerable world he opened up to me at nearly forty miles per gallon. Taking pictures of our destinations became a passion, but I also became fascinated with the places that flashed by outside the car window or we passed through just long enough to trigger my curiosity. It was those places, those small towns, where I wanted to stop, grab my camera, and explore. Unfortunately, I wasn't driving.

Years later, in the spring of 1998, I sat down to plot a great photo expedition by brightly highlighting a Minnesota road map with twenty-six randomly selected towns — one for each letter of the alphabet. My simple criteria were that these towns have a population of under one thousand and be evenly distributed across the state. With only my own agenda to follow, I packed my camera and hit the road in my comfortable old Delta 88.

Off I went, with no set schedule, no plan other than to head for a spot on a map. I envisioned photographing a town inanimate — focusing on buildings and not people. Perhaps I was a little worried about being seen as an outsider exploiting these places with a fancy camera. I found myself on unfamiliar turf, feeling a little self-conscious and awkward, almost sneaking around the first few towns, not wanting to draw attention or suspicion from the locals. "Don't mind me, I'm only here to take pictures of the buildings." What was I thinking? I now find it amusing to see myself wandering around, trying to keep a low profile while lugging a bunch of camera gear that included a stepladder. It wasn't long before the locals approached to ask what I was doing.

The friendly curiosity and subsequent generosity of the first few people I met so impressed me that I found myself rethinking the focus of my entire project. I was received with unexpected and disarming interest and hospitality, and my trepidations began to dissolve as I realized many residents were pleasantly surprised by my desire to photograph their towns. As I progressed on my journey, I began taking the initiative to seek out people and introduce myself. I also began asking if I could photograph them.

Without exception, I was made to feel welcome in every town I visited. People I had just met took me into their homes, offering something to eat and drink. They opened old worn photo albums and spoke candidly of family stories and loaned me collections of written history I never would have found elsewhere. Mayors and maintenance workers unlocked ladders and allowed me to take pictures from high atop water towers, and I enjoyed similar vantages from rooftops and grain elevators. Anglers took me out fishing, old-timers entertained me with stories and beer. I went to ballgames, drove a tractor, and attended a wedding reception. Mine was rapidly evolving as a cooperative project, and many experiences at the time, while seeming diversionary, came to define these towns even more so than my photographs.

Because I met a host of people with whom I shared a great deal, I found myself changing the focus of this text. I originally hadn't given much thought to my writing other than to include a brief historical account of each town. This, after all, was to be a picture book — due in large part to my passion for photography and admitted insecurity as a writer. I have still included a basic historical background for each town, but I have also tried to relate many personal experiences and observations.

"Minnesota Nice" became dynamically different from what I had been used to. I got a sense that the residents of these small towns were more trusting and a little easier to get to know than folks in a big city. I found a certain innocence that has been lost where I live. Children in these towns played freely and unsupervised — I found it interesting to note that not once did I see them wearing any protective gear as they rode their bicycles. Life's pace is a little slower and more deliberate out here, with a greater sense of purpose and interaction in activities of daily life. Things we do anonymously in big cities, such as buying groceries, filling the car up with gas, or making a bank deposit, are often occasions in small towns for conversing with friends and neighbors. Critics of this lifestyle often depict it as boring and affording little privacy. It's ironic that many people would claim to have more privacy in a densely populated city than they would in a small community, and I learned that the price of anonymity is a detachment from the social interactions I saw as so vital to the life of these small towns.

Rural life is no longer as isolated as it once was. Computers and satellite TV have brought us all much closer together. I was surprised at how many people gave me e-mail or website addresses and often found myself sheepishly admitting that not only didn't I own a computer, but I was illiterate in their use. Even though this modern link was shared in every town, important historical links to the past were often slowly disappearing.

Many of these once thriving places are evolving into bedroom communities for nearby larger cities. Newer businesses, churches, and schools coincide with the old, and outer rings of newer homes exist, but much has been lost to changing times and disaster. Fire has consumed many buildings in almost every town I visited. Wood stoves and coal furnaces contributed to the demise of many once stately and ornate wooden structures. In a big city, the loss of a few old buildings would hardly be noticed, but in some of these small towns it often wiped out most or all of the original business district.

Small farms still serve as important extensions of most of the places I visited. Active grain elevators and feed mills remain as reminders of a century-old form of commerce, but their spur tracks often lie overgrown and rusted. Trains no longer stop in most small towns — trucks haul what locomotives once did. Goods that used to be available on every main street are purchased more often in supermarkets and discount stores a short drive away. I met a retired farmer now living in town who reminisced about the days when trains made regular stops, but he had no reason to board. "Everything you needed," he told me, "was right here." I wish that I could have experienced small-town life as it was then. In a certain way, perhaps I did.

Despite spending only a day or two in these towns, I came away with a profound appreciation and understanding not only of rural life but also of the kindness innate in all of us. Over the course of four months, I covered a little more than fourteen thousand miles, stopping in places long enough to satisfy a twenty-year curiosity. I will never forget the experiences and lessons randomly awarded by the open road — and the friends I made along the way.

ON A COOL AND BLUSTERY DAY, I set out for Argyle, a town I knew only as a destination highlighted on the upper left corner of my map. Driving north on U.S. Highway 75, I was taken by the perfect flatness of the land and by the fields of crops I had never before seen in Minnesota — sugar beets and sunflowers. Their light greens and bright yellows contrasted sharply against a gray sky, but conditions were otherwise unsuitable for taking pictures when I arrived in town. With photography on hold, I took a stroll to survey my surroundings and by chance met longtime residents Oliver and Doris LaBine.

The LaBines graciously invited me into their home and served hot coffee and chocolate zucchini cake — the kind I imagined only a grandmother could make. As we talked, I learned that Oliver was president of the Argyle Historical Society, and he offered a private tour of the Argyle Museum which was arranged for a later, sunnier day. This day, however, was spent enjoying the hospitality of my hosts, whose name LaBine is quite common in these parts. Oliver's great-grandfather, born in Quebec, was one of Argyle's first settlers and also one of many French Canadians who located here before the turn of the century.

Ancient glacial Lake Aggasiz once covered this region of the state and left behind rich soil that was promoted in literature circulated in Europe by railroad magnate James J. Hill and his associates. The promise of jobs, cheap land, and farming incentives spurred immigration that contributed to Argyle's growth and that of towns all along the Great Northern Railroad. Argyle was incorporated in 1883 and got its name from Great Northern attorney Solomon Comstock, who proposed the title in honor of a county in his native Scotland.

View from atop the grain elevator at Rivard's Quality Seeds Inc., a registered seed cleaning plant in operation since 1967. Besides dealing in cereal grains and livestock feed, Rivard's produces canary seed that is distributed worldwide.

This retired fire truck received a new door emblem to commemorate the town's centennial in 1983.

Establishment of a potato market in the 1920s led to the construction of Argyle's co-op warehouse.

By 1891, Argyle's culturally diverse population was more than three hundred, and on the streets it was possible to hear seven languages. This year also marked the end of an early period of development. A fire broke out at the town's bakery, and because firefighters were hampered by recent snowfall and bitter cold, many buildings were lost. Undaunted, residents rebuilt, and the blaze was actually credited for stimulating new and more rapid development. Many new buildings were erected of brick rather than wood, and in testimony to the recovery, an 1894 letter in Argyle's *Marshall County Banner* boasted of a diverse business district that included a bank, restaurant, grocery and retail stores, hotels, barber shops, livery stables, saloons, and more.

When bids for the construction of a walkbridge over the Middle River in Memorial Park were prohibitively costly, planners got creative. They purchased an old railroad car for $110 and recruited volunteers to set it in place.

Built as the Argyle Hotel in 1896, St. Gabriel's Apartments provide housing for migrant workers employed in area beet fields.

Oliver LaBine, longtime Argyle resident and president of the Argyle Historical Society

St. Rose of Lima parish was organized in 1879, and this church was built in 1917. Father Henry Rousseau served as pastor here from 1933 to 1971. Masses were said in French for many years.

Growth continued as Argyle moved forward into a new century, and some improvements came faster than others. Electric lights arrived in 1897; the streets were paved seventy years later. Recently, a shopping mall and new bank were built, but Argyle hasn't forgotten its history. The old train depot, converted into a museum, is filled with memorabilia from the town's beginnings. Here I toured the past with Oliver LaBine. I'll remember his kindness and the history he taught me. I'll also remember his wife's chocolate zucchini cake and the socks he was wearing when I took his picture. He wore argyles.

MINNESOTA SUMMERS are comprised of at least two seemingly timeless traditions: road construction and baseball. I'm not exactly sure which roads led me to Buckman, but they certainly weren't the ones I had plotted on my map. Detour after detour finally guided me to my destination — a sleepy little town not far from the geographic center of the state. How fitting it was then to find myself here in the middle of summer, in the middle of road construction, and in the middle of a baseball game.

I followed a procession of cars turning onto the grassy parking area adjacent to Buckman's manicured ballfield and impressive canopied grandstand — a modern wooden structure probably big enough to accommodate everyone in town. Just getting under way was a Little League game between Buckman's team and a team from the neighboring town of Pierz, located seven miles to the north. Boys from these towns are rivals on the baseball diamond, but many share the same classrooms because Buckman's school closed several years ago and students are now bused to Pierz, the larger (pop. 1,014) of the two towns.

As the grandstand filled up, spectators exchanged greetings, some sat together and chatted, young children not too interested in the game ran around and played — it seemed everyone knew everyone else. I had hardly noticed that a game of baseball was under way, but soon my attention was captured by the crack of a bat and the events on the field. During a lull in the action, I struck up a conversation with a gentleman sitting next to me by commenting on how impressed I was with the ballpark. I learned that it was built with proceeds from the sale of pulltabs in area bars.

Buckman's Little League team at bat against their rivals from the town of Pierz

St. Michael's Catholic Church and cemetery. The church was erected in 1902, and with a granite foundation several feet thick, is undoubtedly the sturdiest building in town. Coincidentally, this parish was organized the same year as Argyle's St. Rose of Lima, in 1879.

Looking north on State Highway 25 as it turns into Buckman's main drag

Like many small towns, Buckman has always had a saloon or two, plus varying businesses going back to the pioneering days of farming. Joseph Mischke came to this region in 1871 and is the first recorded settler. With his two sons, he carved a homestead out of a wild landscape and began working the fertile soil. Other settlers followed, including Clarence B. Buckman, who built up an extensive farm while living the life of a country squire. He eventually made a career in politics and served terms as a state legislator, U.S. Representative, and U.S. deputy marshall. When a township was organized in 1874, it was named Buckman, even though there was a disposition among early settlers to name it Mischke.

Today, Buckman is an island in the middle of a vast farmland that was cleared over a century ago by hardworking pioneers. Coincidentally, 1871 marked not only the arrival here of Joseph Mischke, but also the playing of our nation's first professional baseball game in faraway Fort Wayne, Indiana. Watching the Little Leaguers from Buckman and Pierz, I speculated how many kids in small towns across the country were simultaneously engaged in the great American pastime. After the game, I stopped in at Toby's for a beer. Almost hoping I didn't win anything, I bought a few pulltabs — my way of paying admission to a great ballpark in the middle of Minnesota.

THE FIRST THING I LEARNED about Cosmos was that I mispronounced its name. People here don't use the Carl Sagan pronunciation but instead say "kozmus" in referring to their town. A small lesson, I guess, in speaking Minnesotan. Daniel Hoyt, who probably spoke in the dialect of his native New Hampshire, arrived here in 1864 with plans of building a great university. Because he thought such an institution should reside in a worldly place, he proposed that the town be named Cosmos. Unfortunately, Hoyt died in a harsh blizzard shortly after his arrival, and his dream was never realized.

Early evening on Milky Way

A great university town eighty miles west of the Twin Cities never came to be, and instead a community rooted in the more provincial affairs of agriculture arose. Settlers arrived to take advantage of government land sold for $1.25 per acre — a bargain in the days of quarter-section (160-acre) farms. Cosmos began to take shape, but the humble business district remained more or less unchanged until Minnesota Western Railroad service was established in 1922. This transportation link brought prosperity, and Main Street took on a new look. New businesses were built, and the original bank was moved across the street and remodeled.

These were the days of prohibition and gangsters, and on August 20, 1924, residents were awakened in the middle of the night by a terrific explosion — the bank was being robbed. Four armed bandits had blown the safe after cutting telephone and telegraph wires and were preparing to make off with a large amount of cash, including the creamery payroll. Not to be intimidated, men living nearby grabbed their guns and shot it out with the robbers, who fled empty handed.

Since 1969, explosions of a different sort have become a town tradition. Each summer, Cosmos holds a Space Festival to commemorate the first moon walk, and the two-day celebration is highlighted by an impressive display of fireworks. The space theme, however, definitely doesn't end here. Residents seem to have developed a lighthearted association with the name given to this would-be college town, and the evidence is everywhere. Main Street is now Milky Way Street. East-west avenues are named for constellations, and north-south streets take the names of planets. A giant model rocket sits atop the water tower. Stars and more rockets adorn businesses and homes, and the motto of the Starlite Library is "Satellite to Learning." Cosmos, it seems, took its name and ran with it.

I learned about the Cosmos Space Festival during my initial visit, which occurred a few weeks before the scheduled event. At the urging of several residents, I made the return trip, and despite not arriving until evening, I wasn't disappointed. It seemed the whole town had turned out for the celebration, and as the light began to fade from the sky, I joined a crowd headed to the ballfield to watch the fireworks. I struck up a conversation with a few people around me, and when I admitted I hadn't heard of Cosmos until I selected it for my book based solely on its unusual name, a woman looked at me wryly and said, "Didn't you know we're the center of the universe?" Somewhere, Daniel Hoyt was smiling.

The Lietzau Lumber and Hardware Company erected this building on Main Street (now Milky Way) in 1948 to accommodate their expanding interests. Jack Lietzau started building brooder houses for local farmers in 1933 and a year later had thirteen customers. He soon established a successful contracting business that built many houses and farm buildings. With Jack's family involved, the company in its new location sold not only lumber and hardware, but also farm machinery, appliances, sporting goods, and gifts. In 1962 two of Jack's sons added a taxidermy business. Today Jack is retired, and Lietzau Taxidermy occupies all of the old space. This is still a family-run business, which includes the Frontier Era Trade Goods company offering hand-painted feathers, oak water kegs, throwing hawks, animal skulls, claws, various reproductions, and buffalo meat. Many Native American objects are on display or for sale, and the company produces fringed buckskin jackets. Leather and other materials have been sold or rented out for use in several film productions, such as the movie Dances with Wolves.

Local kids fill water balloons at the city park. Luckily, the photographer wasn't a target.

DELMAR HOLDGRAFER IS ON A MISSION. He keeps a keen eye on the skies over Donnelly, ever vigilant of the pesky English sparrow. This aggressive, non-native species has been known to drive out or kill indigenous birds and take over a town, but that won't happen here because Delmar traps and "recycles" the winged offenders. This may sound cruel, but Delmar expresses a genuine passion for conservation. He maintains a number of nesting boxes throughout town in an ongoing effort to propagate Donnelly's population of tree swallows, and he proudly told me that bluebirds are nesting here for the first time in ages. At his home, he showed me nesting boxes for wood ducks that he keeps in his backyard, which borders a dry lake bed filled with wild grasses.

In the 1870s, as pioneers in covered wagons pushed westward in search of Black Hills gold, the territory around Donnelly became known as the sod house frontier. Those settling here had just started a life of farming when the skies turned black with the arrival of Rocky Mountain locusts. They consumed everything in sight — crops, clothing on the line, and wooden handles of farm implements. Masses of the slippery insects blanketed the railroad, and train wheels spun in place until sand could be shoveled onto the tracks. The plague lasted three years, and many people, including Ignatius Donnelly, packed up and left.

Donnelly, however, had lived only part time in the town bearing his name. Though he owned land and farmed here, his career was in state and national politics, and his home was near St. Paul in a town named for his associate John Nininger. The town Nininger went bust, but the town Donnelly survived and grew. New settlers arrived by train, bringing carloads of furniture, livestock, and machinery. A new century dawned and the locusts were

Howard Hennen on his beautifully restored John Deere 1938-B tractor. Hennen is head mechanic at the CENEX co-op and also serves as Donnelly's mayor. He kindly took time from work to go home, start up his tractor, and drive it to the old train depot where he posed for this picture. The depot has been moved from its original location and now stands preserved on the grounds of the town's annual threshing bee.

gone, but farmers faced another problem — too much water. Shallow prairie lakes dotted the flat land, and heavy rains caused fields to flood. To alleviate the problem, workers dug miles of ditches and drained lakes — a common practice on the frontier.

As farmers prospered, so did the town. In 1910, Donnelly had a bustling main street of shops, saloons, inns, an eatery, and a bank. Three churches and a school had been built, and choice corner lots were selling for sixty dollars. Soon, automobiles became commonplace, and stores stayed open late on Wednesday and Saturday nights to accommodate arriving motorists. The Roaring Twenties brought Model Ts and ringing cash registers, but development was short lived. A depression and war were on the horizon, and places like this would never again look the same.

In Donnelly, as in most small communities, many of the young generation have moved away. I was therefore heartened to learn that a young man had come back to his hometown and was running Sax's Cafe. It was here, over lunch, that I first met one of the old generation, Delmar Holdgrafer. I'm glad cafes like Sax's survive. They are often the only places left in small towns where people can meet, socialize, and just possibly learn a thing or two about birds.

Looking over the town from atop the Harvest States grain elevator.

Besides keeping an eye on the town's bird populations, Delmar Holdgrafer writes the "Donnelly News," a weekly column printed in the Morris Tribune. He is also an accomplished artist, and his political cartoons have been widely published.

Myrtle Frank runs the hardware store that was purchased by her husband shortly after World War II.

The old Donnelly State Bank, now home to Tommy's Bar, was built after a major fire swept through town in 1916. Eleven years later, the bank was closed, and its interests were acquired by the Farmers and Merchants State Bank, which has been in business since 1912.

The Donnelly Super Market presently occupies this building, but the sign out back still advertises Lee Overalls.

EFFIE LIES AT THE NORTH END of the most beautiful stretch of highway in Minnesota (my opinion of course, but after traversing fourteen thousand miles of state blacktop, I can't think of a finer drive). The morning was weather perfect as I steered onto State Highway 38 at its south end in Grand Rapids. I was soon free of civilization and on a smooth ride of random pitch and direction. A forest thick with pine and poplar was interrupted only by the ribbon of road and clearings of shimmering lakes. Not realizing I'd been gaining elevation, I passed over the watershed divide. Now I, too, was flowing toward Hudson Bay, still on a course not for an inch either flat or straight. Eventually I was spit out onto an open landscape of farms and level fields. I wanted to go back and do it again, but Effie was waiting.

What I found was a sparse little town marked by a single flashing traffic light and the biggest mosquito I've ever seen. The imposing insect is actually a monument erected next to a welcome sign that advertises Effie as an edge of the wilderness community. This territory is infamous for its mosquitos, and Effie seems to subscribe to the old notion that if you can't beat 'em, join 'em. I parked at the Effie Cafe, a restaurant I thought conspicuously large for such a small community. As I got out of the car, I was met by the ominous stare of a big wooden mosquito perched on the side of the building. During the course of my leisurely lunch, it became evident that not just locals dined here. This is the only eatery for miles, and it's a popular stop for tourists and truckers.

State Highway 1 runs east-west and for a short stretch provides Effie with a main street. Traffic on this road has right-of-way, and heavily laden logging trucks are a common sight as they rumble through town headed for mills in International Falls or Grand Rapids.

Effie's school has closed, but the old hockey boards remain. The building is now home to the Little Dipper Company, bottlers of pure drinking water.

Many a tourist has been photographed in Effie lying under the giant stinger of this mosquito. There's no word on whether or not anyone has actually been bitten.

A logging truck rumbles past the Effie Cafe on Highway 1. Effie is named for the daughter of early postmaster Cap Wenaus.

Truckers bound for Grand Rapids opt to detour west of Highway 38, avoiding what I'm sure would be a harrowing ride in a big rig. But the Mack trucks of today serve merely as reminders of the large-scale operations of a different era. Lumber companies located downriver on Lake of the Woods bought up tracts of virgin pine in this area, and by 1880 the logging boom was under way.

Creeks, rivers, and lakes were soon choked with freshly cut timber that lumberjacks urged northward under often difficult conditions. As logging camps sprang up across the region, a township soon took shape. In 1912 Effie became a station of the Minneapolis and Rainy River Railway, and mountains of logs were moved to new markets by rail. But the focus of commerce shifted as settlers established homesteads and groomed cleared land for farming. By the 1930s, evidence of the lumber boom began to disappear — even the railroad tracks were pulled up. Today the Effie Cafe stands about where the old depot once did. Despite its beginnings, Effie has always been a quiet little town. This truly is an edge of the wilderness community, even though the mosquitos aren't quite as big as advertised.

The Effie Cafe is open seven days a week, serving locals and travelers alike. The place is packed on Friday nights for the all-you-can-eat walleye dinner.

The Effie Country Service advertises milk, pop, bait, groceries, and ice cream. It also provides gas, twenty-four-hour towing service, and a full line of auto repairs.

This popular watering hole is located on the site of the old railroad siding, where trains once loaded mountains of freshly cut timber.

FREEBORN IS SO UNASSUMING that its road signs don't even list the town's population (301 according to my highway map). This is an old community — platted in 1857, a year before Minnesota entered the Union. One of the members of the first Territorial Legislature was a rugged leader by the name of William Freeborn, and it is for him that the town, an adjacent lake, and the county they lie in are named. The county borders Iowa and is known for holding some of the state's richest soil.

I came to Freeborn on a warm autumn day when most of the traffic in town revolved around the Terra grain elevator. Harvest was under way, and as tractors and combines hauled their hoppers in, fully loaded eighteen wheelers rolled out. It was hard for me to imagine that this region's open farmland was once covered with tall prairie grasses and hardwood trees, which must have been even harder to clear than the conifers of the north. On the east shore of Freeborn Lake, a large stand of old trees is preserved in Arrowhead Point Park. In the earlier days, a bathhouse stood here, and many people would gather to swim and bathe in the shallow waters.

One of the town's first landmarks was a huge mill built in 1867 on the north shore of the lake. A wheel of wooden sails nearly fifty feet in diameter drove the millstones that provided early settlers with flour — provided the wind was blowing. Unfortunately, the wind blew too hard one day in 1875, and the wheel was destroyed, never to be rebuilt. The mill house was razed twenty years later. I found drawings of the old mill and other historic buildings at the Freeborn Grocery. The informative sketches were part of a school project and hang on a wall behind a table reserved for the lunch crowd. While here, I was encouraged to pay a visit to a town historian of sorts who lives just a couple of blocks away.

In 1919 four districts were merged to create a consolidated school at Freeborn. This building was completed in 1922 and serves as an elementary school. Freeborn's older students attend high school in the town of Wells.

Tracy Christensen has spent a lifetime in this area. Her husband Marvin has too. They married in 1940 and farmed just outside of town for many years. Even though they now live in a newer rambler in town, it wouldn't be fair to call them retired. They are both very much active, and Tracy has worked tirelessly since 1980 to locate and document all

Philip Cichos moved to Freeborn from North Dakota in the 1930s. He maintains a welding and repair shop next to his home where he can fix just about anything. Not surprisingly, his old Ford tractor still runs like new.

An eye-level view of Freeborn's water tower from atop the Terra grain elevator

Marvin and Tracy Christensen at the Melander School. The Christensens have been instrumental in restoring the one-room school-house, which was built in 1878.

Corner of 5th Avenue and Park Street. The Freeborn Grocery got its start nearly a century ago as Anderson's store, which at one time also provided space for a bank, doctor's office, and drugstore.

The restored Melander School

of Freeborn County's old school districts. At one time, there was a schoolhouse every few miles or so — a total of about 145 were built. Tracy has extensively researched all of the districts and has photographed the schoolhouses still standing. Her living room doubles as an office, complete with fax and copy machines.

As rural towns grew and school districts consolidated, the old one-room schoolhouses became obsolete. Through the efforts of the Christensens, however, one such building has been preserved in Freeborn. The old Melander school (named for John Melander, the farmer on whose land it sat) was moved to a park in town in 1954. Restoration started years later and is now more or less complete. Entering the doors, I was sent back in time by the old desks, books, wall maps, and antique wood stove. To the Christensens, the school is still a work in progress. To me, it's a reminder of the importance of historic preservation and the ambitions of good people.

IN THE 1890s, the Red Lake Indian Reservation was reapportioned by the U.S. government, and waves of immigrants, mostly Scandinavians and Germans, spread out over newly surveyed lands to establish farms and villages. In a lowland area along the banks of the Lost River arose a new settlement called Wildwood, where a busy sawmill provided lumber and jobs, and Main Street began as a narrow dirt road lined with a few rugged storefronts. As the village grew, the Lutherans erected a church and local farmers organized to build a creamery. Then the railroad arrived, creating quite a dilemma.

When the Soo Line came through in 1910, the tracks were laid on higher ground, away from the community. Realizing the importance of being next to the railroad, Wildwood basically moved up the hill and started over. When a post office was needed, an application was sent to Washington, but a reply came back stating that the name Wildwood was already taken in Minnesota (I found a town named Wildwood just west of Effie). It was then decided to name the town for early Norwegian settler Martin O. Gonvick. With trains providing regular service for freight and passengers, the newly named community grew rapidly. Businesses flourished along a relocated Main Street while new roads were being forged for the automobile.

In the early 1920s, a route was completed through town that stretched all the way from Winnipeg to New Orleans. The unpaved Jefferson Highway was advertised as the "All-the-Year Vacation Route of America, From Pine to Palm." A description of the route stated that "In its course the Jefferson not only traverses the heart of the richest country on the globe, but also one filled with romance and sentiment." The stretch that once passed through Gonvick has long since been replaced by State Highway 92, which today runs right by the high school football field.

The Wildwood apartment building bears the name of the area's original settlement. The building was constructed in the 1920s as the Gonvick Banner print shop after a previous facility on the site was lost to fire. Later the building served for many years as Gonvick's post office. A new post office was erected next door.

During my first visit to Gonvick, I happened to pick up a schedule for the high school's upcoming sports season. It was tucked into my camera bag, and I came across it several days later while staying at a friend's cabin some 150 miles south. The school's homecoming football game was coming up, and I decided to make the return trip to catch the action. I figured it would be worth the extra miles, and a fun way to wrap up my swing through the state's northwest. So I packed the car, drove out to a familiar highway, and turned north once again. I was going to a Bears game.

On a warm evening, I showed up at the playing field and joined a short line at the admission gate. Noticing my camera gear, the woman selling tickets asked if I was a member of the press, and before I could provide an answer she waved me past. I worked my way through a lively crowd until I reached the steps of an elevated press box. Thinking "what the heck, I'm press," up I went. The crew inside welcomed me aboard just as the Clearbrook-Gonvick Bears took the field against the Red Lake County Central Mustangs. With the sun setting on a pastoral landscape, I kicked back to watch the game and take a few pictures. Call it Wildwood or call it Gonvick, on this evening I had come to just the right place.

Behind the stands at the homecoming game.

Main Street in Gonvick. Down a hill at the end of the street lies the Lost River and the site of the village of Wildwood.

In a town named Gonvick, it seems only natural to have a cafe named Ole & Lena's.

The Gonvick Mercantile now does business in a former grocery store. The Mercantile sells clothing, footwear, and assorted novelty items. Next door is the office for Winsor Products Company, makers of that famous Norwegian delicacy — lefse.

Vandy's Country Market looks nothing like the old store from which it has been reshaped. Originally built in 1909 as the two-story Gonvick Mercantile, the building lost its second floor when renovated in 1958.

BEING ON THE ROAD for a while was making me feel a bit disheveled so when I rolled into Halstad on a hot August day, I came to a simple realization — I needed a haircut. Driving around town in search of a barber shop proved to be fruitless, but I figured a community of six hundred residents must have someplace to trim all those heads of hair. After asking around, I was directed to a newer home at the edge of town. There, through a private basement entrance, was Patty's Beauty Shop. Patty runs a modern full service salon, and she kindly squeezed me in between appointments of a couple regular clients. "Cut it short," I requested, and soon I was feeling like a new man and out exploring the town.

I took a stroll down 3rd Street, past CG's Liquors and Cassie's Cafe, past the MeritCare medical clinic and Holland Hardware store, following a curve in the road that led me to a riverbank. This is the edge of town and the edge of Minnesota, where 3rd Street crosses an old narrow bridge and disappears into North Dakota. Here flows the border, the Red River of the North. I stood staring, almost in disbelief, at the seemingly harmless trickle of water that lay before me. It had been a long, dry summer, and the river was so low I figured I could almost wade across. It was hard to imagine that this was the very same river that had wreaked so much havoc on this part of the country.

Much has been documented on the terrible flooding during the spring of 1997 when the Red came out of its banks and swallowed up millions of acres of countryside. Many towns, large and small, were drowned as well. Halstad was one of the few places in the river's path that escaped relatively unscathed — thanks to permanent dikes that were built around the town in the 1960s. Because most of the town stayed dry, local volunteers were able

Halstad's main row of business is on 3rd Street, shown here looking east toward Highway 75.

to fill hundreds of thousands of sandbags for neighboring towns less fortunate. For as long as people have been living in this area, coping with floods has been a way of life, but the river has brought prosperity as well.

Steamboats were plying the Red's waters as far back as the 1870s, bringing passengers and freight to various stops along a route from Fargo to Winnipeg. The narrow river made for often difficult navigation, however, which was only compounded when water levels were low. Winter freeze-ups suspended travel for months, and by the end of the century the steamboats were but a memory, replaced by the ever expanding railroad. Ironically, steamboats played a role in the railroad's formation, ferrying everything from steel rails to locomotives.

When Ole Halstad settled in this area in 1871, ox carts provided the most reliable, if not always the fastest, means of transportation. Halstad established a post office in his home, and it is for him the present town is named. What started as a sparsely populated township eventually gave form to a growing village that was incorporated in 1892. Since then, Halstad has matured into a modern, close-knit community — one whose bond is only strengthened by the ravaging forces of a sometimes fickle river.

The post office faces 2nd Avenue, once known as Main Street. Next door is a building that was moved from across the street in the late 1920s to replace a meat market lost to fire.

Unusual for a town its size, Halstad has its own medical clinic. The building was built in 1916 as the First State Bank and replaced the original bank destroyed by fire a year earlier. Halstad also boasts its own dental center.

Looking into Minnesota and the outskirts of Halstad from North Dakota. A new bridge is being constructed upriver of the old bridge that has been periodically battered by floodwaters since 1933.

An old elevator and its newer replacement, which can be seen in the distance

A school bus view of Norman County West High School. Although partially obscured by a newer addition, the old Halstad High building of 1905 still stands.

DESPITE BEING A MINNESOTA RESIDENT my entire life, I've caught a grand total of exactly one walleye. That sobering fact was on my mind as I drove down the west shore of Mille Lacs Lake on a perfect sun-drenched afternoon. A perfect afternoon, I thought, for fishing. Perhaps I would have time finally to test the waters of the state's second largest lake and haul out one of its renowned inhabitants. My trusty rod and reel were packed into the trunk, just in case.

I continued along my route as it bent with the shoreline, turning east until I reached my destination — the town of Isle. As I climbed out of the car, I was welcomed to Main Street by a giant fish replica that boasts Mille Lacs as the "Walleye Capital of the World." I was eager to validate that claim for myself but wanted to explore my surroundings first. What I found were busy streets lined with quaint businesses and resorts, sidewalks scattered with meandering vacationers, all of which suggested a town that felt touristy, yet not overly commercialized. This is the biggest town on the lake, and it's come a long way from the slow beginnings of a bygone era.

Settlers began arriving on the southeast shore of Mille Lacs in 1891, taking advantage of a partly enclosed bay and the natural shelter provided by Malone Island. The island, which is actually more of an isthmus bordering one side of Isle Harbor, got its name from Charley Malone, who was the first to establish a business here. He built a general store and hotel in 1894 and owned title to the island, which he originally named for his daughter Ethel. When he was appointed postmaster, Malone suggested that the town be called Ethel's Island, but the name was subsequently shortened to its present form.

Isle's museum contains many interesting displays, plus an impressive collection of artifacts and old photographs from the Mille Lacs area.

From its perch just off Main Street, this giant walleye welcomes visitors with a slogan often heard in these parts.

First opened in 1992, Susi's Norskehus is one of Isle's newer businesses. The hard-to-miss gift shop is located in the building once belonging to Isle's first newspaper, the Advance.

The building now housing Lake Country Gifts (blue awning) originally served as a hotel.

Main Street as seen from the offices of the Mille Lacs Messenger, a weekly newspaper that is distributed throughout the lake region. The Messenger began in 1928 with the merging of the Isle Advance and the Onamia Herald.

The Francis Resort's launch sits ready to take another party of anglers out onto Mille Lacs. Although several other species populate the big lake, the walleye is the most sought after.

Logging was the major industry in the early days. As the surrounding forest of white pine was cleared, much of the timber was transported by rail to nearby Knife Lake, where it was floated down a chain of rivers all the way to sawmills in Stillwater. When the region's economy inevitably shifted to one based on agriculture, Isle was still a tiny, relatively undeveloped village. But the 1920s brought new highways and the area's first vacation cabins. Tourism fostered rapid growth, and a town emerged. A few of Isle's older resorts are clustered at the end of Main Street, where they still maintain an active business.

It was mid-afternoon when I wandered over to the Francis Resort at the edge of town. This wasn't exactly the best time of day to fish for walleye, and the resort's launch sat quietly tied to the dock. The evening excursion was hours away from departing, but I got permission to go aboard and look around. The big pontoon boat was fully equipped for dozens of anglers, and a sign on a window read "Bait Boy works strictly for tips, Thank You for your kindness." Ultimately I never had time to fish while in Isle. I will return, however, and when I do, I'm signing up for a trip on a launch. A full-service, guided excursion seems like the way to go, especially for someone like me, who is unfamiliar with the lake. I want at least to double my lifetime catch of walleye — and I'll take all the help I can get.

JASPER IS A TOWN CHISELED FROM STONE — literally. Many of its buildings, notably those comprising a rather substantial business district, are built from a quartzite known as jasper. Mining of Jasper's distinctively pinkish rock began in 1888 — the same year the townsite was platted on the line between, fittingly, Rock and Pipestone Counties. A period of remarkable growth gave rise to a community that less than a year after its inception boasted a population of two hundred residents and dozens of businesses, and no business was bigger than the quarry operations. Although tons of building blocks were turned out for local use, production centered on cobblestones, and huge numbers were shipped off to new markets by rail.

Unfortunately, cobblestone production was soon terminated because it was discovered the stones became highly polished with wear and caused treacherous footing for horses. Fortunately the ultra-hard quartzite proved to be suitable for other uses. After the outbreak of World War I, U.S. metal producers used jasper to replace previously imported German silex as a grinding stone for mineral dressing (separating metals from their ores). As metals were conserved as part of the war effort, jasper also replaced iron and steel as a lining material in the ore mills and in mills generating other products as well.

Marketed under the name Adamant Silica, Jasper's quartzite was widely distributed throughout the country during the course of World War I. It was used at the U.S. Powder Mill in Old Hickory, Tennessee, for instance, where production of gunpowder reached a million pounds a day. Ironically, the same quality that made the quartzite so unsuitable for cobblestones has proved to be invaluable to its ongoing success as a medium for mill linings

The girls' softball team took the field against their rivals from nearby Garretson, South Dakota.

and grinding cubes. Besides being essential in metal-ore processing, the rock is utilized in making a variety of products, including salt, paint pigments, talcum powder, fertilizer, and pottery materials. Many industries rely heavily on jasper, and in Minnesota's aptly named town, mill-lining blocks and grinding cubes continue to take shape from a quarry that began over one hundred years ago.

The Jasper Stone Company is an unmistakable landmark that lies just at the edge of town. The superintendent, Curt Johnson, kindly agreed to let me wander around his vast operation. Upon promising to heed his advice not to fall and hurt myself, I was free to explore. Starting on the company's lower level where the finishing work is done, I made my way past buildings where rough blocks of stone are broken apart by massive electric saws and hydraulic splitters. I learned that not all work is done by machine, however, and watched as workers wielded hammers and chisels in the ancient practice of stonecutting. After walking up a road to the upper level, I encountered a crew excavating large slabs of jasper at the edge of the quarry. Although the excavation process is often tough and backbreaking, the men I talked to seemed to be content with their work and proud to be part of an ongoing tradition — a tradition from which their very town is built.

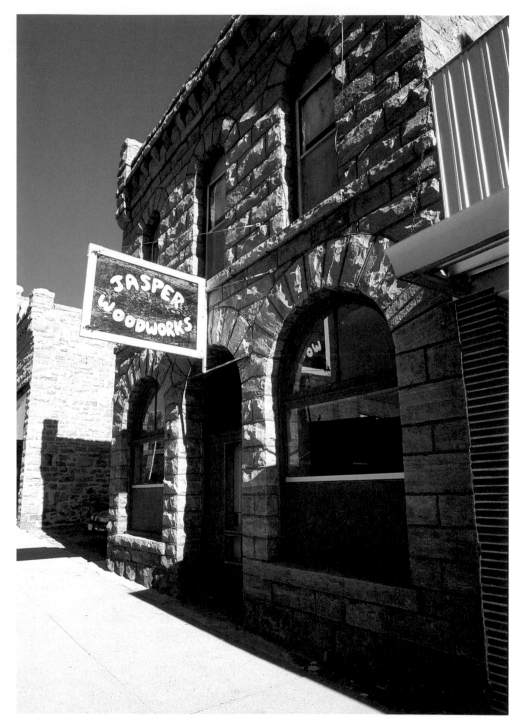

One of Jasper's oldest stone buildings. Note the rough edges of the blocks, which were used for making buildings only after they were deemed unsuitable for other purposes that required more precise cutting.

Jasper is often used in the milling process that produces many of the materials that go into making ceramics, including those once sold at this closed down gift shop.

Early evening on Wall Street. This main road cuts through the center of town and is lined with many old stone buildings.

The Jasper Stone Company was placed on the National Register of Historic Places in 1979. Here workers excavate large slabs of jasper from the company's quarry.

The old wood structure at Jasper Yards seems almost out of place in this town where so many buildings are made of pink quartzite.

A VERY FAMOUS PERSON was buried in Kelliher, Minnesota, on June 25, 1955. In a park at the edge of town, under a conspicuously large burial mound, lies Paul Bunyan himself — or so they say. When the residents here dedicated Paul Bunyan Park, they "buried" the mythical logger and erected a small headstone with the simple epitaph "Here lies Paul, and that's all." To make things official, they obtained a burial permit from the Minnesota Department of Health. Apparently, there really are bones buried at the gravesite, at least according to the folks I met at Bradley's Cafe. I was told that the grave contains ox bones, which caused me to wonder if they might be those of Paul's famous blue ox, Babe. I didn't ask, however, figuring some things are better left to mystery.

While at Bradley's Cafe, I also learned that I mispronounced the town's name (as I did with Cosmos). The proper pronunciation here is "kelly-er", which I never learned whether or not matched the way Jerry O'Kelliher referred to himself. O'Kelliher was a prominent lumber company agent, and when the town was founded in 1903, it took his name (most of it anyway). The town of Kelliher was nurtured by the lumber companies and the railroad, and a colorful history is evoked by many of its old names — names like Cash Murphy, Stuttering Jack Gillis, Black Erick, Hungry Mike Sullivan, and Protestant Bob.

Old businesses, gone but not forgotten, tell of an interesting past as well. In the 1920s, Eggen's Cafe and Bakery was a popular spot where locals gathered to eat, converse, and sip the trademark egg coffee. The Pastime Theater delighted patrons with vaudeville shows, boxing matches, and silent movies. During the same era, the Kelliher Hotel often overflowed on weekends with lumberjacks eager to spend some time on the town.

State Highway 72 runs north from Kelliher all the way to Canada and has to be the loneliest stretch of road in Minnesota. Tiny Waskish, on the shores of Upper Red Lake, is the only other town for fifty-five miles.

Through the years, the big, double-winged building also housed a poolhall, bowling alley, creamery, and production facilities for the *Kelliher Independent*. The old hotel stood as the town's greatest landmark until it unfortunately burned to the ground in 1971.

Fires and attrition have claimed a fair share of Kelliher's past. Today the town bears little resemblance to the one portrayed in the old black-and-white photos that hang in the Citizens State Bank. The elegant bank, in fact, is among the few old businesses left. There's also the Beck Lumber Company, which dates to the turn of the century, and the Kelliher Shopping Center, which began as a general store in 1910. In recent years, a new post office, a senior center, and several new businesses have been established, including Thor's Sports Bar and a couple of gift shops where one can buy this area's latest cash crop — wild rice. Despite all its changes, Kelliher has remained an active little town. Many people have spent a lifetime here, and some old-timers can still recall a few of the town's characters. I learned that Cash Murphy was an agent at the old train depot, and Protestant Bob — well, as I thought earlier, some things are better left to mystery.

Raymer and Louise Hoyum were married in 1943 and moved into this house in 1948. They have raised five children in Kelliher and remain active in preserving the town's history.

The old auditorium is used only for storage these days. Built in 1936 by the Works Progress Administration, the building at one time also housed Kelliher's city offices.

Ron Heim (left) and his high school students are building an addition to the Log Cabin Crafts gift shop. Heim teaches a building trades class at Kelliher Community School, and works with the townspeople to provide free labor for various construction projects.

The Roadrunner is closed from fall to spring, but during the summer locals and travelers alike make it a popular spot for grabbing a bite to eat.

Kelliher probably has more churches per capita than any other town I visited. There's Emmanuel Lutheran (pictured here), Our Savior's Lutheran, Grace Presbyterian, St. Patrick's Catholic, and a Church of the Nazarene, for a total of five — or one for every seventy residents.

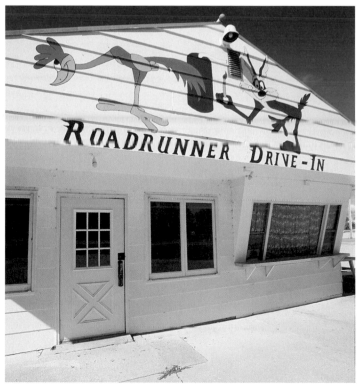

ON FEBRUARY 17, 1998, Alex Trebek of the game show *Jeopardy!* gave a panel of contestants this clue: "Longville, Minnesota, is the capital for racing these reptiles; the slowest compete for the Grand Slowpoke title." The answer, of course, is "What are turtles?" Longville officially became known as the turtle-racing capital of the world when the state legislature passed a resolution declaring it so in 1989. The tradition of racing turtles here, however, dates back to 1967 when a local bar owner came up with the idea as a way to raise money for the Little League baseball team.

Longville is located in one of the most popular resort areas in the state, and every Wednesday during the summer, hundreds of people converge on the little town for the races. I had been previously unaware of this ritual, and it was only by dumb luck that I arrived here on race day. At first I thought the town was holding some kind of street fair because Main Street was blocked off to cars and was crawling with people. After parking in a makeshift lot at the edge of town, I made my way toward the action and said to the nearest person, "This place is a zoo, what's going on?" In response I was told, "It's like this every Wednesday — the turtles are about to race."

On the street, hundreds of kids were busy picking out what they hoped would be a fast turtle from the turtle vendors — local kids who round up the critters from nearby Girl Lake. Participants may supply their own turtles, but most opted to rent one for two dollars (plus a two-dollar refundable deposit). After standing in a long registration line, the kids were ready for action and waited anxiously as groups of ten were called to the race circle painted in the middle of the street. I wanted to take a few pictures so I joined the first heat just before the turtles were released from the center.

Turtle vendors provide hundreds of racers each week. Turtles must have a shell at least four inches long to qualify for competition.

Each Wednesday afternoon during the summer, turtles are given free reign over Longville's Main Street. Longville is named for its first postmaster, James Long.

And they're off! As the announcer calls the race, contestants scramble to the edge of the race circle and urge their racers to victory.

A couple of contestants show off a turtle that looks to have winning form.

When the racers were released, ten kids all ran to the circle's edge and tried coaxing their charges to follow, and I was left standing there in the middle with my camera. A race judge began waving frantically at me because I was obstructing her view, so watching where I stepped (and feeling a little self-conscious), I quickly exited the circle. If I had been registered as a racer, I would have been an easy winner.

By the end of the afternoon, racing was concluded for another week, and prizes for fastest and slowest turtle were awarded to the champions. Cars were eventually allowed back on Main Street, but the sidewalks remained crowded with meandering vacationers. As I wandered about, I got the sense that this is by every definition a tourist town, and one look at the local vacation guide explains why — the chamber of commerce lists more than fifty businesses here. Longville has definitely come a long way from its beginnings as a turn-of-the-century logging camp, and for thousands of kids every summer, it truly is the turtle-racing capital of the world.

Kellogg's Northwoods Sport & Gift Shop sells all kinds of goods, including cream and butter fudge made right behind the front counter.

From Longville's public landing at the eastern edge of Girl Lake, boaters can access a chain of waterways that also includes Boy River, Woman Lake, and Child Lake.

OF ALL THE TOWNS highlighted on my map, Miltona was the only one familiar to me when I set off across the state. Since my youth, I have come here on occasion while staying with neighbors at their vacation homes on nearby lakes. Miltona shares its name with the largest lake in the county, but it is actually a mile or so from the nearest water, so even though I had been in town before, my visits had been brief. I was therefore eager to return. It would be good to spend some time with old friends at the lake, but I also wanted to rediscover a town that had faded into childhood memory.

After spending a restful night in familiar surroundings, I showed up in town at precisely 10 A.M. — that's when a group of locals gather for their ritual games of dice over coffee and a few laughs at the Miltona Grocery. I had witnessed games of chance in many towns I had visited, but this would be the first time I participated. "Shaking for coffee" is what they call it, and that's what we did. Things happened pretty fast, but I think the object was to roll a certain combination of numbers and not be the last one to do so, or something like that. I'm not about to admit being a slow learner, so let's just say I was unlucky, and the coffee was on me.

When the games ended, I made my way along the west side of Main Street and its single row of buildings (the east side of the street is lined by railroad tracks). The outside air was already warm, and over at the VFW hall I walked through the propped-open door and encountered my former neighbor Jerome Haggenmiller, who now lives with his wife Nancy on the shores of Lake Miltona. It was Tuesday, state primary election day, and Jerome and his fellow election judges were taking advantage of a lull in the voting to eat an early lunch. We

Main Street's Club Miltona was built after the tornado went through in 1970. The town is named for Florence Miltona Roadruck; she and her husband were early homesteaders.

visited awhile but the sight of hamburgers was making me hungry, so I headed next door to Club Miltona to get one for myself.

As I ate, I looked around at the modern, sprawling bar and restaurant and was reminded of a dark chapter in the town's history. Club Miltona stands where the Corner Cafe and Dance Hall once did. It was built after the previous structure was destroyed by a tornado on July 18, 1970. The twister cut a swath right through town, heavily damaging all but two businesses. Many homes were also wrecked, and five residents were hospitalized, but fortunately there were no fatalities. With the help of neighboring communities, Miltona's residents banded together to rebuild, but some of the town's old landmarks, like the train depot and grain elevator, were lost forever.

I spent the rest of the day wandering the streets, chatting with residents and taking a few pictures. By sundown I was hungry again and headed back to Club Miltona for dinner. Later on, Jerome came by to join me for a couple beers after his long day over at the VFW. He told me the turnout of registered voters in Miltona Township had been over 80 percent. That figure, more than anything else, attests to the high level of community involvement I discovered in all the towns I visited. Miltona is a great example of a tightly knit community and one I briefly felt part of — even though I never quite got the hang of shaking for coffee.

Jerome Haggenmiller, accompanied by his dog Maggie, fishing on Lake Miltona, the largest lake in Douglas County

Mount Calvary Lutheran Church, built in 1942

Local kids point out their location on a map painted on the playground at the Miltona Science Magnet School. The school, formerly Miltona Elementary, is attended by kids from all over the area who show aptitude in science.

A group of morning regulars "shaking for coffee" at the Miltona Grocery

Don Mattocks returned home on his lawn tractor after voting in the state primary elections. He voted at Miltona's new Fire Station, which served as the polling place for town residents. Residents of rural Miltona Township cast their ballots just down the street at the VFW Hall.

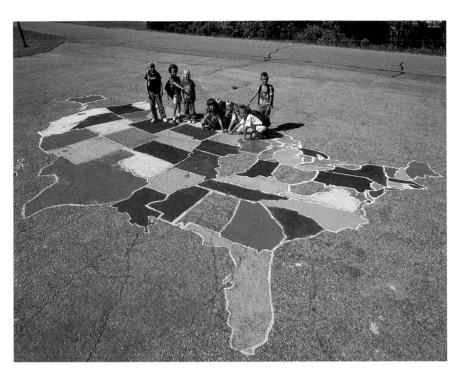

WHILE DOING RESEARCH for this book, I found much information in small publications residents had put together about their own towns, and no such publication was easier to find than the one I discovered in Nicollet. When I drove into town on a hot afternoon, I was tired and thirsty so I parked in front of the Cabin Bar and went in for a Coke. As I paid the bartender, I explained to her my purpose and inquired about local history. What she did next still amazes me. She reached behind the cash register, pulled out a booklet titled *History of the Village of Nicollet, Minnesota, 1856-1970*, and plopped it in front of me. She then wrote down her address and trusted me to mail it back — I didn't even have to ask.

Nicollet, like the county in which it lies, is named for French geographer and explorer Joseph Nicollet, who mapped this area in 1838 (Minneapolis has an island and a street named for him). "Old Nicollet" was platted in 1857 and consisted of a stagecoach station, hotel, church, blacksmith shop, and sawmill, but the entire site was abandoned after only three years because of the foreclosure of bank loans. The present townsite was platted nearby in 1874 after the arrival of the Winona & St. Peter Railroad sparked renewed promise for the area.

Nicollet soon became a viable railroad town, and in 1900 the population was 330. Because of its proximity to the growing cities of St. Peter, Mankato, and New Ulm, passenger trains made frequent stops at the busy depot. Since rail travel was still a novelty, early residents taking even short trips often had their names printed in the society page of the *Nicollet Leader* (another newspaper, printed in German, was also published at the time). Stockyards were built near the tracks, and in 1914 the Nicollet Shippers Association was

Corner of Third and Pine. The building to the right was built in 1905 as Olson's general store; living quarters for the Olson family were upstairs. Several businesses have operated in the old building over the years, but today it stands mostly vacant. A close look at the rear roofline reveals damage caused by recent high winds.

The first Nicollet State Bank was organized in 1903 with a stock capital of ten thousand dollars. In 1922 the bank moved to a new building, shown here.

Gerhardt and Esther Schmidt at the award-winning meat market they started in 1947. The family-run business attracts regular customers from all over the area and even neighboring states.

Lenard Rudenick, at the Nicollet Farmers Exchange grain elevator, is retired from many years of farming and now lives in St. Peter.

Swan Lake, located just outside of Nicollet, is part of one of the most ambitious wildlife projects in state history. Millions of dollars have been spent to acquire lands and manage natural resources in an effort to revitalize the lake and surrounding area, which suffered from years of neglect and abuse. The ten-thousand-acre lake, once sterile from farm run-off, has been restored as a waterfowl mecca and is the largest prairie pothole marsh in America. One supporter of the project is the Nicollet Conservation Club, whose clubhouse sits on the lake's southeast shore. Although hunting is allowed on the lake, some sections are off limits and designated as a game refuge to preserve this beautiful wildlife habitat for many years to come.

organized. Livestock and grain were shipped by rail until the 1930s when trucking became common. Eventually the railroad died out, and though the stockyards are long gone, one of the town's old elevators, at the Nicollet Farmers Exchange, is still operating today.

I met the manager of the Farmers Exchange, Glen Hopp, and he agreed to let me go atop the elevator to take a few pictures. Leading me inside, he asked if I'd rather climb a series of ladders or go up in the man lift. He pointed to the second choice, a small platform the rider self-propels, using rope and pulley, up through a shaft. Feeling adventurous, I chose the man lift. The instructions were pretty simple — stand on a small knob on the floor of the platform to release the brake, then pull to go up. Gravity takes care of the descent. After I gave him a ballpark figure of my weight, Glen removed a couple ballast weights, and up I went. After taking a few pictures, I tried to get down. I stepped on the brake and didn't budge. I jumped on the brake and still didn't budge. I tried pulling up again and only managed to cinch the contraption closer to the ceiling. Apparently I had overestimated my mass and needed those ballast weights. I eventually descended by pressing my hands against the walls of the dark shaft and pushing myself down inch by inch. Exhausted and not wanting to admit my misadventure to Glen, I merely thanked him and left. Figuring it was time for a break, I headed back to the Cabin Bar to study a little history.

ODESSA IS ONE OF THOSE PLACES the highway doesn't visit. This is a quiet community, nestled against the Big Stone National Wildlife Refuge, where tall prairie grasses still grow and buffalo once roamed in endless herds. A. D. Beardsley, who managed the Milwaukee Railroad depot here in 1879, is credited for being the first settler and opening the first general store. Odessa's name can be traced to three different origins: A. D. Beardsley's daughter Dessa, early settler John Desso, and the city in Russia from which early farmers imported seed wheat. A town sprang up at a curve in the tracks, and although the railroad fostered the creation of grain elevators, lumber yards, and a flour mill, it also brought tragedy.

In 1911 a fast moving silk train (named for its cargo of imported silks) rounded the bend unable to brake in time for the Columbian Flyer parked at the depot. It was the middle of the night, and the Flyer's rear sleeper car was fully occupied — the collision killed eleven people. A freight train derailed at the bend in 1957, and a similar accident happened ten years later. When I arrived in town, I met many residents who were all too familiar with these accounts.

I had missed the breakfast crowd at the Mud Hen Cafe, but a few locals strolled in as I was grabbing a bite and thinking about my plan of action. Having learned it made sense to photograph eastward facing streets in the morning, I made a habit of surveying a town to note the compass orientation of interesting buildings. I wanted to catch the early light, but the new arrivals were providing good conversation. Figuring the sun could wait, I hung out for awhile.

Just before high noon, with my camera at my side, I set out to drive around the town. I was accompanied by the postmaster, who conducted a quick tour that ended at the

In 1902 Richard Menzel built a lumberyard bearing his name. Over the years he bought out three competitors, expanded the business, and added a hardware store. Credit was often extended for a year to early settlers, allowing them time to erect buildings and reap crops. Everyone needed lumber, and surrounding county schools purchased maple flooring scraps for use as kindling in their stoves. Chip Menzel, who began working here as a young man just out of high school, inherited his father's business, but it is now closed.

post office because he had to get back to work. Not much remained of the old business district for me to photograph, and as I pondered my next move, I encountered LeRoy Strei, one of Odessa's old timers, who had pulled up to mail some letters. I mentioned that I had heard about a local legend of sorts by the name of Cliff Olson and found myself following LeRoy a few blocks to his friend Cliff's house. Cliff often sits in his truck and watches the world go by, and he was doing just that, in the company of his neighbor Emil Van Erem, when I pulled up on the gravel road in front of his house.

Retired from operating a mink ranch, Cliff has a rare hobby that has brought attention from across the country. He is a wheelwright — he makes and restores wooden wagon wheels, buggies, and sleighs. LeRoy, Emil, and I followed Cliff to an old outbuilding to behold a collection of forgotten vehicles standing in testament to a time before motors. Aging hands have slowed his efforts, and Cliff seemed somewhat apologetic as he removed dusty tarps to uncover works in progress. I was nonetheless impressed by his craftsmanship and by his spirit. Spending the afternoon with these three men was an unexpected treat, and they showed me that sometimes a town's most interesting subjects are its people.

The names Kollitz and Menzel are significant in the history of this community. Herman Kollitz opened a general store in 1883 and four years later moved his prospering business into a newly constructed building on a corner of Main Street, where his sons continued his interests until 1971. After a period under new ownership, the store closed, but it remains standing today as a reminder of the old-fashioned service that once included sending a bag of jelly beans with weekly grocery orders.

Cliff Olson and an example of his old-time craftsmanship

Lunchtime at the Mud Hen Cafe

Justin Moen and his dog, Bodo. Ellingson's Inc. has been in business in Odessa since 1952, producing honey from its considerable colonies of bees. Justin works across the street at Triple D Wax Rendering, where he melts honeycombs for beeswax.

Three retired old timers: (left to right) Emil Van Erem, former supper club owner, Cliff Olson, wheelwright and former mink rancher, and LeRoy Strei, who delivered mail on a rural route and ran a family produce business

PALISADE GOT ITS START when a railroad span was built over the river here in 1910. When I entered town, I drove past a large wooden sign that reads "Welcome to Palisade on the Mississippi," then went down to a county park and campground that lie in the shadow of the old trestle bridge. Though it was the first of October and the air was refreshingly cool, the leaves had not yet turned. I sat watching the old river, thinking about how it would eventually wind its way to my hometown of St. Paul and waiting so I might take a picture of a passing train. None appeared, however, and I gave up my watch and drove over to Main Street.

I went into the Palisade Cafe where I soon learned it was a good thing I hadn't waited too long by the river. Trains haven't come through town in quite awhile; in fact, the tracks no longer exist and the rail bed and bridge are now part of a year-round recreational trail. During the winter months, snowmobiles are a common sight in Palisade, and when the town holds its midwinter festival in February, Main Street is lined with hundreds of the machines, some belonging to members of the local Super Sledders Club.

After lunch, I met Ralph Fowlds, who was sitting on his porch as he does most afternoons. An octogenarian, he has lived in Palisade his whole life. He farmed in the area many years and last worked at the creamery, which is no longer in operation but still standing across the street from his house. When Ralph told me that later in the day he would be going a few blocks to the municipal bar on Main Street for happy hour, he said he would be going "uptown" — a reference I had heard in quite a few towns, mostly from old timers. I told Ralph I might just meet him uptown and went off to see more of Palisade.

I found pairs of at least a few businesses. Besides the Palisade Cafe, there is also

Located on the Mississippi River, Palisade got its start when the railroad was completed here in 1910. Railroad officials named the town for the palisades, or riverbanks.

On a farm at the edge of town lies this interesting piece of field art made from an old cable spool.

Bethany Beck poses with a few Palisade pumpkins on the first day of October.

View from atop the old co-op feed mill, which is no longer in service. The building is now used for storage.

Ralph Fowlds relaxing on his porch, as he does on most days. Ralph has lived in Palisade for more than eighty years.

Wayne Dreher sits at the counter of the Palisade Cafe, which he recently bought after moving to Palisade from the Twin Cities. The cafe is one of the oldest buildings in town and was recently expanded to accommodate increasing business.

the Our Family Homestead Kitchen (old photographs of the town adorn the walls at both places). Across Main Street from the municipal liquor store and bar is another bar, Patty's Beef & Beer, a modern place that was once an auto-body repair shop. Also on Main Street are two gas stations. There are three churches in town, including Assembly of God, which many years ago served as a movie theater. It didn't take long to tour this town of 144 residents, and I soon found myself back where I had started, at Berglund Park.

Knowing I didn't run the risk of meeting any approaching trains, I walked up an embankment and out onto the old bridge. I watched the river again, this time thinking about the steamboats that used to maneuver between the narrow banks hauling settlers, loggers, and supplies to the two dozen or so landings that existed along this stretch between Aitkin and Grand Rapids. I heard that some of the old sternwheelers were still in service after the bridge was built and could pass under it only after their hinged smokestacks were folded down. I stood looking down on the river for a long time, wishing there was more color in the trees and thinking about the past. And when the sun began casting long shadows, I climbed down the embankment and went off to meet Ralph. As he would say, I was headed uptown.

THERE IS ONLY ONE Minnesota town name that begins with the letter "Q", and with that in mind I started off one day to find Quamba. State Highway 23 runs diagonally across Minnesota from its southwest corner to Duluth, and on the stretch between Mora and Interstate 35, I shot right past the "Quamba pop. 124" sign without seeing any evidence of a town. Knowing that finding an alternate town wasn't an option, I doubled back, looking a little more closely. I noticed a lonely road and a few buildings just north of the highway so I turned off, crossed the railroad tracks, and found what I had been looking for.

The Great Northern Railroad built a siding here in 1882, but for many years the present townsite was nothing more than a train waterstop, known then as Mud Creek. When a town was platted in 1901, railroad officials changed the name to Quamba in reference to the shallow waters of nearby Mud Lake, where local Ojibwe grew wild rice (the name most likely is derived from the Ojibwe word "gwaaba," meaning "to scoop up"). Of the first settlers to arrive, most were Swedish immigrants, and their native language was spoken extensively in the new town. In fact, many of Quamba's first schoolchildren spoke only Swedish so kids from a neighboring town were brought into their classes to help them learn English.

Jonas Olson opened Quamba's first general store in the early 1900s, signaling the start of a small business district that today has all but disappeared. A bank was opened in 1917, only to move to Mora fifteen years later. S. S. Patterson owned a lumberyard here but, under new ownership in 1953, it was also moved to Mora. The hardware store built by Ole Nystrom in 1920 survived many years but eventually closed. Even the old post office is gone. But in spite of all the economic decay, new construction has taken place. In 1991 the Quamba Baptist

Beatrice Haines on the porch of the Happy Haven foster care home, an assisted living residence for seniors.

Church dedicated a new building that replaced the old schoolhouse the congregation had used for seventy years (the old building still stands and is used today as a youth center).

Quamba is the only town I visited besides unincorporated Yucatan that doesn't have a single public establishment, such as a bar, cafe, grocery store, or gas station, and because of that I had a hard time meeting any residents. After stopping here four times over the course of my travels, my persistence paid off. I met Linda Oquist, who with the help of her husband, Dean, and daughter Karen, runs Happy Haven, a foster care residence that provides assisted living services for seniors. The Oquists live upstairs in the old building, formerly Jonas Olson's store. I spent some time on the front porch one evening, socializing with the Oquists and a couple of their neighbors and tasting Dean's homemade strawberry wine. As we sat and talked, a boy roared past on a noisy dirtbike and a few cars went by bringing people home from work elsewhere (before it closed a dozen years ago, people would have stopped across the street at Cougarville, a supper club named for the pets kept out back by the owner). One of the foster residents, Beatrice Haines, joined me on the porch swing and talked about the old days. She also recited some beautiful poems she had written about the wonders of nature, changing seasons, and faith. That evening, on the porch at Happy Haven, Quamba became much more than a lonely road and a few buildings.

Quamba's schoolhouse was built just after the turn of the century and became the home of the Quamba Baptist Church when a new school was completed in 1921. Seventy years later, a new church building was dedicated, and the building found new use as a youth center. An area youth group, "Short Horses," is named for ponies that a student minister from the Twin Cities noticed en route to Quamba.

The Quamba Cubs belong to a local recreational league. Players are high school age and older.

The legend of Elvis lives on in Quamba. A local girl bought the sign and erected it on her street, naming it for her idol.

Residents regularly gather to discuss community affairs at city hall, which also serves as a polling place during election years.

"UP NORTH" SEEMS TO BE a common term in this state and one generally used to reference anything between the Twin Cities and Bemidji. Anything north of Bemidji, I've noticed, often gets referred to as "way up north." That said, I found myself one day driving way up north to Roosevelt, located only a few miles from Lake of the Woods, which contains the Northwest Angle and the northernmost point in the contiguous forty-eight states.

Roosevelt, organized in 1907 and named for President Theodore, was once surrounded by great stands of timber. Today most of the old-growth forest is gone, logged out years ago by the many lumber companies that operated sawmills here. When I drove into town, I found little evidence of that bygone era and discovered instead a quiet community of a few narrow streets and a main block of exactly three buildings: Knutson's Hartz store, the post office, and the city office. I stopped at the post office, where old photos on the wall gave a few glimpses into the past. Catching my eye was a faded image of an old train depot, built in 1905. I assumed the building had been torn down because I hadn't noticed it while driving through town, but I learned it had been moved a few miles from its former location and converted into a residence. Unfortunately the fate of other old buildings wasn't so encouraging. Many, including a cafe, hotel, tavern, and apiary, were lost to a major fire in 1945.

Next door to the post office is a grocery store, the town's oldest surviving establishment. Built in 1909 as Lars Oseid's general store, it is operated today as a Hartz store by Gene Knutson, Roosevelt's mayor. There are a couple hundred individually owned Hartz stores in rural communities throughout Minnesota and North Dakota, and Mayor Knutson told me his was one of the busiest. As we talked, several people came in to shop,

Looking south along Roosevelt's main street. The brick building, now a Hartz store, was originally Lars Oseid's general store.

Trains on the Canadian National Railroad skirt the south end of Lake of the Woods, passing through Roosevelt on their way between Manitoba and Ontario.

Gene Knutson, Roosevelt's mayor and proprietor of Knutson's Hartz store.

Marty Spenst and Mark Mickewicz pause on "Old 11," a residential street that was part of State Highway 11 until that route was moved just south of town. The long metal building in the distance houses Roosevelt's public skating rink.

Marty Spenst and Mark Mickewicz pause on "Old 11," a residential street that was part of State Highway 11 until that route was moved just south of town. The long metal building in the distance houses Roosevelt's public skating rink.

World War I claimed a significant number of men from Roosevelt's small population; those who died in the service of their country are listed on this memorial.

backing up his claim. Groceries have long been the staple of Knutson's business, but in keeping with the times, he also stocks scores of rental videos. The mayor chatted for awhile with his customers and me, then excused himself to attend to official business.

Actually I never found out whether the mayor was acting in some official capacity or just as a friend, but his business was to visit a local woman who had been bitten by a woodchuck. It had gotten into a bag of rabbit food and nipped the woman when she reached inside. Concerned about rabies, she contacted Knutson to trap the rodent so that it might be tested. I guess in a small town like Roosevelt, you can't call Animal Control so you might as well call the mayor.

After buying a snack at the Hartz store, I went for a walk around town. Past the city office and down a narrow side street, I came upon a long metal structure resembling a pole barn. It was Roosevelt's indoor public skating rink. Though it isn't heated, the attached warming house is, and I learned the facility sees a lot of use during winter months. This is, after all, hockey country. Out on the highway that runs past town, cars whizzed by, heading to places like Baudette or Warroad, where Roosevelt kids go to school. I was soon on that highway myself, leaving behind the northernmost town on my journey. I didn't leave behind "way up north" for many miles, however. Not until, I think, somewhere around Bemidji.

FOLLOWING THE ARRIVAL OF SETTLERS in the 1870s, the wild prairie of Cottonwood County gave way to fields of wheat and oats. Most of the new arrivals were of Scandinavian descent, and many lived in dugouts until more permanent structures could be built. Legend has it the Reverend J. C. Jacobson, an early circuit minister, was out walking one day and paid an unexpected visit to the Holman family; he fell right through the roof of their dugout home. When the startled family asked where he came from, his simple answer was, "I came from above."

Reverend Jacobson helped organize a township that eventually became known as Town of Norsk, and a post office was established with that name. In 1875 a simpler title was proposed, and the name was changed to Storden to honor the Norwegian town of Stord. Some confusion still exists over the name Storden, which apparently was interpreted from the reference "Stord, in Norway." The first settlements in the township were Hoyt, Amo, and Copenhagen — towns that were bypassed when the railroad was built in 1899. It was therefore decided to start a new town near the tracks, and construction began on grain elevators and lumberyards. Existing buildings from Copenhagen were moved to the new location and joined a growing number of newly built homes and businesses. Like the township, the new town was named Storden.

Soon after the turn of the century, significant growth put Storden on the map to stay. In 1903 telephone service was established when a line was connected to the C. H. Shaner general store, and the township government provided many other improvements, including gas lights and wooden sidewalks. Electric service started in 1920, the same year Storden was incorporated. With the election of public officials, led by businessman turned mayor

One of Storden's equine residents in a pasture at the edge of town. In the background is the elevator of the Farmers Grain Company, whose history dates to 1906.

Local volunteers contributed the furnishings for the restored Hystad cabin.

Saturday afternoon on America Street. A very HOT Saturday afternoon, according to the sign on the Heartland State Bank (71 degrees Celsius equals 160 degrees Fahrenheit).

The Storden Township building serves as a meeting place and as a storage facility for road maintenance equipment.

Longtime Storden resident Marian Hart in front of the Shady Drive Inn, named for the shade provided by a large cottonwood tree that grows adjacent to the building

This old fire engine has long been retired from service in the Storden Fire Department, which was organized in 1921. The town's first alarm system consisted of a used school bell that was purchased for $3.75.

O. C. Lande, the town began a government independent of the township. Today Storden perseveres as a small yet active community whose stability is evident in a few of the old businesses still in operation. The *Times/Review* weekly newspaper began publishing in 1900, and the bank has been in operation since 1904. Most notable is the Westbrook Mutual Insurance Company, which since its start in 1889 has become a major provider, serving scores of policy holders throughout southwest Minnesota.

Although some of the town's past has been preserved in its businesses, I found an interesting example of pioneer history that began a hundred miles north of here. Nestled among the tall grasses and wildflowers of Storden's tiny Native Prairie Garden lies an old log cabin that was transported to its present site in 1996 after being donated by the town of Sunburg. The cabin was built in 1866 by Norwegian immigrant Nels Hystad and has been restored and turned into a museum by volunteers in Storden. Many artifacts grace the interior, and a guest book on a corner table lists visitors from across the country. I was amazed to learn the building remains open and unattended, twenty-four hours a day from spring until fall. I also learned that nothing has been tampered with and thought about how special that is nowadays. Preserving 130 years of history anywhere is a noble thing, and in Storden it means just a little bit more.

IT OCCURRED TO ME when I rolled into Taunton late one afternoon that the town's original name of Lonesome seemed somewhat appropriate. There were a couple of cars parked in front of the Corner Cafe, but with the bank and post office closed for the day, Main Street was more or less deserted. I wandered up Main, past a couple weathered storefronts, and stopped to take a few pictures of a neat white building I assumed was the town hall. It wasn't long before an older gentleman walked over from his house across the street to find out what I was doing. With a smile and a handshake, he introduced himself as Duane Sarbaum, and I explained my project.

Duane told me the building facing us was indeed the town hall but hadn't been used as such since a new hall was recently erected. The old building had been restored and converted into a senior center. Duane asked if I wanted to look inside. After walking back to his house to get the keys, he returned, with his wife Marian, and gave me a tour. The Sarbaums seemed proud the almost-one-hundred-year-old-building was still serving the community.

Back at their house, the Sarbaums served refreshments and gave me a copy of Taunton's centennial history booklet, published in 1986. Duane pointed out a story about two former residents credited for inventing an improved and safer railroad-car coupling mechanism. Printed along with the story was a copy of the patent, issued to Minnie McPhail and Frank Kopicke in 1894. As I perused the town's history, I also came across a story about Sts. Cyril and Methodius Church that included a photo of Marian seated at the church's pipe organ. She began playing for Sunday services at age eleven and continued as the organist for sixty-one years.

The feed mill and grain elevator (in background) of the Taunton Cooperative Elevator Company, which began as the Farmers Cooperative Produce Company in 1912.

Now retired from her long tenure at the church, Marian still volunteers to perform once a week at a nursing home in nearby Minneota and regularly plays the organ she keeps in her living room. As she rendered a few hymns for me, I was impressed by her smooth and flawless style, which was especially notable because she was using only her left hand. At age fourteen, she lost the use of her right hand after suffering from accidental poisoning, and has been playing one handed since. With evening approaching, I had to say goodbye to my hosts and leave Taunton. I had a previous commitment elsewhere and told the Sarbaums I would return another day. Duane walked me to my car, and with another handshake, thanked me for coming.

When I returned a few weeks later, the town had a different feel from that on my first visit. On State Highway 68, or First Street, there was activity at the co-op elevator company, Taunton's center of commerce since 1912. People were out and about on Main Street, and the bank and post office were both open. In the Corner Cafe, a group of old timers were playing gin rummy and talking about changes their little agricultural community has weathered over the years. Out on the street, I encountered Duane and Marian as they pulled up to the corner stop sign in their car. Duane rolled down the window to say hello and explained they were leaving town for the day. I watched them drive off, thinking about how wonderful some of my chance encounters had been and about how one town had seemed so deserted until a stranger came over to say hello.

Bethlehem Lutheran Church was built in 1886 but has stood unused since the congregation disbanded in 1981.

Duane and Marian Sarbaum in front of the senior center, formerly Taunton's town hall. The Sarbaums have lived in the same house across the street since their marriage in 1949.

In 1886 the first post office here was established under the name Lonesome. That name was soon changed to Taunton in honor of a city of the same name in Massachusetts.

Angling northwest from Marshall to Canby, State Highway 68 becomes First Street as it passes through Taunton. The building to the right is the Corner Cafe.

Inside the Corner Cafe, a group of longtime residents gathered for a few games of gin rummy.

IT HAD BEEN A LONG TIME since I attended an early morning church service, but after my first visit to Upsala, I returned to do exactly that. During my first visit to this self-proclaimed "Minnesota's friendliest little city," I was taking pictures from the lawn of a stately white church when a man on a riding mower buzzed past me and waved. On the next pass, he throttled back to idle and hollered that I should go inside and take a look. I went over and introduced myself to the man, who works as caretaker of the church, and learned the fate of the old building was shrouded in controversy over rumors that some parishioners wanted it torn down and replaced.

Inside St. Mary's Catholic Church during Sunday mass

The caretaker was animated in describing his reasons for preserving the church, which has quite an interesting history. It was built in 1914 in the little town of St. Francis, four miles south of Upsala, and moved to its present site in the winter of 1954. Known originally as the Church of St. Francis of Assisi, it was renamed St. Mary's. The relocation involved placing it on steel beams and dollies and slowly maneuvering it, using six trucks, down a frozen road. Overhead wires and mailboxes along the route had to be moved aside, and the total cost of the move was five thousand dollars. The building was free — it was donated by the congregation in St. Francis to make way for their new church.

After taking a look inside, I contacted Father Gregory, a young man who had just been appointed St. Mary's pastor, and arranged to return the next Sunday to take pictures during a service. A few days later, I awoke at the crack of dawn and drove back to Upsala, arriving at the church about a half hour before the scheduled 8:00 A.M. mass. From the balcony, I looked around at the ornate altars and stained-glass windows and watched as the

congregation filtered in. The air in the church was warm and still, and most of the parishioners were dressed casually. I'm sure a modern, air-conditioned church would have been more comfortable, but I knew the caretaker was right — the aesthetics of old St. Mary's could never be duplicated.

Until St. Mary's was moved here, Upsala had been without a Catholic church since its beginnings in the 1880s. The town's first settlers were predominantly Scandinavian Protestants, who built Lutheran and Baptist churches and named the settlement for the university city of Uppsala, Sweden. As the town grew, German and Polish Catholics arrived, but without a church of their own they had to travel a few miles to neighboring towns for mass.

Today Upsala is home to five churches, as well as a public K-12 school, library, senior citizens center, and city park. The Upsala Area Historical Society, formed in 1979 for the purpose of saving the town's old REO fire truck, operates the Borgstrom House Museum on Main Strret. The museum, which was donated to the society, holds a wealth of artifacts dating to the early part of the century. Upsala seems dedicated to preserving its history, and for the time being, St. Mary's appears to be safe. Father Gregory told me the diocese isn't in the habit of tearing down servicable churches, which seems to be a pretty sensible policy. And one I'm sure many, including the caretaker, appreciate.

East side of Main Street. The Uptown Cafe is a popular spot for an after-church breakfast. The motel advertised on the cafe's sign is the small building next door and has recently closed.

Posters advertising the Fourth of July celebration were still tacked up all over town when I arrived here on July 9.

Pastor Gregory Mastey greets members of the congregation after conducting mass at St. Mary's. Father Gregory also serves as pastor of St. Edward's Church in Elmdale, a town of 130 residents that lies a few miles east of Upsala.

The Trustworthy General Hardware store is one of the oldest buildings in Upsala. It was built as a general store in 1905 and at one time had a movie theater upstairs (now an apartment).

Looking south on Main Street, which is also State Highway 238, a short and crooked route running between Interstate 94 at Albany and Highway 27 just outside of Little Falls

WHILE IN VERGAS, I had the opportunity to do a little fishing so I stopped at Big Jim's bait shop at the edge of town. The place was locked up, however, because Jim was on vacation. The back door, though, had been left open to allow patrons access to a small room where live bait is kept. Transactions were handled according to the honor system; a sign instructed customers to tally up their purchases and deposit monies through a slot in the wall. Cramming a couple of dollars into the overflowing slot, I paid for some worms, then left with a smile on my face. It felt good being trusted by Big Jim.

Vergas is surrounded by lakes and lies adjacent to Long Lake, which is where I headed to fish from the public pier. The pier is part of a community park best known for its loon statue, a towering landmark that has fixed its gaze over the waters since being built in 1963. After a productive afternoon fishing, I dined at the Loon's Nest, a popular Main Street eatery dating to 1940. Minnesota's state bird is a common theme in this town; every summer Main Street hosts a weekend-long Looney Days festival that offers a range of activities, including a parade, craft sales, games, and of course, a loon-calling contest.

In a flier that advertises a number of local merchants and resorts, the Vergas Community Club touts "Minnesota's Finest Tourist & Vacation Area," but it was logging and railroading that put Vergas on the map. Organized in 1903 as the village of Altona, the town got its present name in 1906 from Soo Line Railroad officials. At the time, sleeping cars that traveled on the Minneapolis to Winnipeg route were designated as the "V" series and were named Venlo, Venus, Viking, and Vergas. The name change was made because Altona was too easily confused with another Soo Line town, Miltona (also covered in these pages).

Paige Saunders poses with her father, Jon, in front of the Vergas Loon before trying her luck fishing at Long Lake. The Saunders family hails from Manilla, Iowa, and vacations regularly near Vergas.

Vergas's Main Street is lined with a variety of businesses, including gift shops that cater to vacationers from the surrounding area. The blue building in the center is the Loon's Nest Restaurant.

This giant map facing Main Street advertises no fewer than twenty-four resorts in the immediate area.

Big Jim's is more than a bait shop. Patrons can also throw in a load of laundry and grab a bite to eat before venturing to the lake.

The United Methodist Church was built in Pelican Rapids in 1886 and was moved approximately fifteen miles to Vergas in 1911. It was transported in sections across frozen lakes by horse-drawn logging sleds.

Among the first businesses in many new railroad towns were dray lines, or transport services. With trains bringing a range of cargo, from coal and lumber to personal furnishings and farm machinery, draymen filled the important role of delivering these goods throughout new communities. As Vergas was established, residents relied on drayman David E. Brooks and his teams of sturdy work horses. Brooks's teams worked year-round pulling wagons and sleds and were also hitched to scrapers for digging cellars and making roads. With Ford Model T trucks eventually replacing his horses, Brooks continued doing business until the late 1930s.

The town Brooks helped shape at the beginning of the century has changed a lot over the years, and today it boasts an array of businesses that belie its modest population of less than three hundred. Gently sloping Main Street is home to a bank, realty office, restaurant (the Loon's Nest), bar, beauty salon, and stores selling hardware, liquor, antiques, gifts, and groceries. Supported by the surrounding vacation area, Vergas has a healthy economy and benefits from the experienced leadership of mayor Roger Hanson, who has served terms in Minnesota's House of Representatives and Senate. Hanson and his family have been active in the local business community for many years, and at the edge of town sits one of his "biggest" triumphs — the loon he was instrumental in bringing to the shores of Long Lake.

WINTON IS SITUATED ON FALL LAKE at the edge of the Boundary Waters Canoe Area and got its start during the early days of logging. In 1892 Samuel Knox came here from Wisconsin, where he and his brother William had established numerous logging camps and lumber mills. Attracted to northern Minnesota's vast expanse of timber and numerous waterways, he built a mill on a scenic peninsula of Fall Lake, and his operation became known as the Knox Lumber Company (not to be confused with the chain of home-improvement stores that started in St. Paul in 1961). The Swallow and Hopkins Lumber Company began operations on the opposite side of the peninsula a few years later, and together these two mills attracted hundreds of workers, most having just arrived from Sweden and Finland.

With an influx of laborers and their families, a boom town was born, and folks named the new community Winton in honor of Billy Winton, Sam Knox's business partner and son-in-law. They rapidly built businesses, boardinghouses, and private homes, and erected a community center known as Finn Hall, where stage plays, dances, lectures, and classes in English and naturalization were held. New industry arrived in 1910 in the form of commercial fishing, and companies began harvesting whitefish, lake trout, pike, and walleye from nearby Basswood Lake. Daily catches reached two tons, and a large refrigeration and storage plant was built. The additional jobs pushed Winton's population to an unofficial high of two thousand, but the heyday didn't last long. Only ten years after they began, the fisheries were closed as new laws prohibited the commercialization of game fish. With a depleted supply of timber, sawmills were dismantled. As Winton's population declined, deteriorating buildings were razed and many houses were jacked up and moved to Ely.

St. Louis County Road 118 becomes Third Avenue as it winds into Winton. At left is the old town jail and to the right, a residence, formerly McTaggart's Pool Hall. According to local folklore, there once was a man in town, known as quite a gymnast, who would perform for drinks by standing on his nose atop a pool table.

Jim Donahue runs the only bait shop in the area.

The Fat Chicken Feed Store and the post office occupy this old train depot, built in 1912, where residents in years past could board a train to Ely for a fare of five cents.

Noted conservationist Sigurd Olson once owned this outfitting company. It was built as a lumber company horse barn and now stands in possession of the U.S. Forest Service.

Ellefson's Saloon once stood on this corner that now provides space for a playground.

Today Winton is home to fewer than two hundred residents. When I arrived in town, I met one of them, Jim Donahue, who runs the Winton Bait Shop. Jim provides for anglers heading out onto Fall Lake, but it's not the busy point of entry to the surrounding expanse of water that it once was. The BWCA Wilderness Act of 1978 restricted motorboat use on area lakes, and in compensation for lost revenue, the U.S. Forest Service has purchased resorts, outfitters, and private land. As Jim and I talked about fishing and the changes that have affected his business, I hoped to do a little fishing myself, but an impending storm dictated otherwise.

After leaving the bait shop, I walked around town until drops of rain forced me to take shelter in my car down by the shores of Fall Lake. Big thunderstorms can seem even more awesome in a wilderness setting like Winton's, and strong winds soon toppled

trees, snapped power lines, and drove the rain sideways as I sat in nervous appreciation of Mother Nature and thought about lumberjacks stuck on log drives many years ago during similar conditions. I was obviously through exploring Winton for the day and unfortunately couldn't stay until the next. So when the rain stopped, I headed for another town, wishing I could have seen a little more. And as I drove through Ely, I paid special notice to older homes and wondered which ones came from just up the road.

O.K., SO THERE ISN'T REALLY a Xylophone, Minnesota. The "residents" pictured here are actually guests, neighbors, and the owners of Olstad's Resort on Lake Miltona in Douglas County. These folks agreed to help me out after I explained that since Minnesota doesn't have a town that begins with the letter X, I had been looking for a way to create one. A journey from A to Z shouldn't skip a letter, after all. After taking this picture, I became curious about what it would take to actually incorporate a town in this state. Here's what I found out.

Guests and neighbors of Dewey Olstad (in the red shirt) and his wife Janet Olstad (center), owners of Olstad's Resort on Lake Miltona in Douglas County.

Incorporation is overseen by the state Municipal Board, which consists of three governor-appointed members who serve six-year terms. For such proceedings, two county commissioners from the county where the affected land is located also serve on the board. To initiate proceedings, one hundred or more property owners residing within an area can file a petition, or in other circumstances, an existing town board that has jurisdiction over the land in question can file a resolution. The land can't be within the limits of an already incorporated town, and some of the land must be platted into lots and blocks according to law (which doesn't require any specific amount of land to be platted, by the way).

A copy of the petition or resolution must be sent to the executive director of the Municipal Board (who doesn't serve as a member of the board itself), containing the proposed name of the town, the names of all parties entitled to receive a mailed notice under the law, the reason for incorporation, and a map showing the proposed boundaries of the area to be incorporated. A public hearing is then held by the Municipal Board, which considers a variety of factors including number of households, projected growth, land features, intended development, and transportation. Existing levels of governmental services

(water, sewer, street maintenance, fire protection, law enforcement) are also considered, as are fiscal and school district matters.

If everything meets the test for incorporation, a board order is issued, and a document is filed with both the secretary of state and the county auditor. Once the residents of the newly incorporated town elect their government, the town goes on the map. It's as simple as that. So who knows, with eighty-seven more residents and a little paperwork, Xylophone might actually become a real town some day.

"A BUFFALO WALKS INTO A BAR . . ." That may sound like the beginning of a joke, but it actually happened in Yucatan, an unincorporated hamlet nestled in a valley amid the rolling hills and trout streams of Minnesota's driftless area — the southeast corner untouched by glaciers that leveled the rest of the state thousands of years ago at the end of the Ice Age. Settled in 1852 and named for a peninsula in Mexico, Yucatan is a sparse, rural community of farms and a few buildings lining a gravel road. The road, designated by a homemade sign as Main Street, leads to the Yucatan Supper Club, where I knocked on the door and met Suzanne Crossman. Inviting me inside, Suzanne explained she and her husband closed the business a few years ago and were in the process of converting the building into their residence. She offered some interesting background on the place, which was built as a general store more than a hundred years ago, and showed me a collection of photographs depicting an unusual encounter.

On a summer day several years ago, a handful of customers occupied the supper club as Suzanne worked behind bar. When a shadow suddenly filled the room, Suzanne turned and looked but couldn't believe her eyes as a man with a real, live buffalo in tow entered the room. The man lived nearby and had previously joked about bringing his tame buffalo in for a beer. The buffalo, named Cody, had an impressive resume that included various promotional appearances and work in the movie *Dances With Wolves*. The photos Suzanne showed me were of herself and Cody posing at the bar and of his owner feeding him motivational treats — Oreo cookies.

After Suzanne related her fascinating story, we were joined by her husband, Toby,

Beautiful Yucatan valley is located in Houston County, which covers the southeastern corner of the state.

who arrived home from work. Out back, he showed me a group of animals he and Suzanne raise as a side business. The strange looking creatures were emus, probably more rare to the area than even buffalo. Wondering what else Yucatan had to offer, I thanked the Crossmans and wandered across the road to inspect a one-room schoolhouse. The small, white building sits on private land next to a large garden and is known as the Store School because of its proximity to the old general store. It was used until the 1950s, at which time students were transferred to a school in the nearby town of Houston. I found the Store School relatively well preserved, especially considering its age; it was built during the Civil War.

The Store School, however, isn't the oldest schoolhouse in Yucatan. A couple miles up County Road 4 lies the Stone School, named for the material of which it was constructed in about 1860. The thick-walled school is as solid as ever, but its name seems to be deceptive because a wooden facade was added to the building not long after it was built. Today the building is the Yucatan Town Hall. The two schools are undoubtedly the oldest buildings I came across during the course of my journey, and I was surprised to find them in the most obscure and least populated place I visited. Then again, Yucatan is full of surprises. Just ask anyone who happened to be in the supper club when a buffalo walked through the front door.

The Store School has been abandoned since the 1950s.

The Yucatan creamery was built in 1905 and sits on the farm of Pete Solberg, shown here with his dog, Bailey. Pete's grandfather was the buttermaker here from 1920 until the last year of production — 1963.

The first interment at the Yucatan Cemetery was in 1873. Among those buried here are veterans of the Civil War whose service to the Union is eulogized on their grave markers.

I HAVE ALWAYS BEEN FASCINATED BY AIRPLANES, so when the Wicker Woman of Zumbro Falls told me about a project she had recently completed, I was intrigued. The Wicker Woman is Cathryn Peters, who runs a wicker-restoration and chair-caning business out of a century-old Main Street building originally used as a newspaper print shop. Her contribution to aviation involved crafting wicker seats for a replica of a 1929 Sikorsky S-38 amphibian plane that was recently piloted by Sam Johnson, chairman of the S. C. Johnson Company, in an attempt to re-create a journey made by his father in 1935. Flying an S-38, Sam's father had traveled round trip from Milwaukee to Brazil to study the Carnauba palm for its use in making the company's wax products.

Cathryn was kind enough to show me around her studio, where she also teaches basketry classes and sells wicker crafts and antiques. She is active in historic preservation and provided me a copy of the 1998 Zumbro Falls centennial booklet. The one-hundredth birthday was celebrated in conjunction with the springtime Ripplin' River Daze Festival, named for the Zumbro River, which flows through town. The river hasn't always been a cause for celebration, however. On numerous occasions over the years, the Zumbro has spilled over its banks, causing widespread damage and washing away all but a few traces of the grist-mill dam that once created the falls for which the town is named.

The grist mill was built in 1866 as original development took place on the south side of the river. This settlement dates to 1857; it grew quickly into a thriving community of private homes, two churches, a hospital, and several businesses, including a hotel and ferry service, but flooding and a tornado eventually prompted relocation to higher ground on the

Cathryn Peters, otherwise known as the Wicker Woman, in front of her studio, which was used as a print shop for Zumbro Falls's first newspaper, the Independent

The Zumbro Falls school was built on a hill high above town in 1913 and replaced a previous school destroyed by a tornado. In 1980 the school was closed, and students were transferred to Lake City.

Looking west on Main Street, or State Highway 60

The Broadway Restaurant building started out as a saloon in the early 1900s and became a hardware store shortly thereafter. It remained a hardware store until 1980, at which time the present business was established.

An older residence on the east end of Main Street is decked out for Halloween. Next to the home is the fire department and city hall, erected in 1980 and 1992, respectively.

north side of the river. The "new" Zumbro Falls benefited from the arrival of the railroad in 1881 and was incorporated in 1898 (the original settlement exists today as a small residential area).

Most commercial development in the new location took place on Main Street's north side, away from the river and at the foot of a steep hillside. Several turn-of-the-century buildings remain, giving Zumbro Falls a distinct old-town appearance. The former Doty hardware store, constructed of locally quarried stone in 1878, is the oldest surviving structure. It was recently renovated, having stood empty and in disrepair for many years, and is now home to Norm's Bar, one of three watering holes along Main Street, or State Highway 60, a popular summertime motorcycle route that passes through the heart of Wabasha County.

The last leg of my journey began when I drove out of Zumbro Falls on Highway 60 and headed for St. Paul. After four months of traveling, I looked forward to going home, but I also felt like a kid who wants to hear just one more story before going to bed. I had exhausted the alphabet (not to mention all of my film, money, and clean clothes) but not my curiosity. There are hundreds of small towns across Minnesota's 87,000 square miles, and I couldn't help feeling that I had only scratched the surface.

Index of Towns

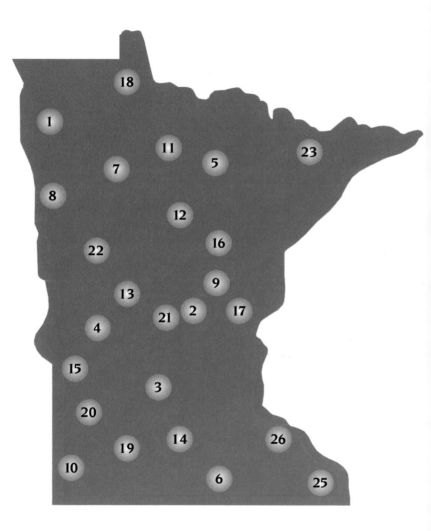

Acknowledgments

FOR THEIR HOSPITALITY and contributions to this book, I would like to extend heartfelt thanks to the following people: Oliver and Doris LaBine, and Ken Schuster from Argyle; Jeanette Janson from Buckman; Jack Lietzau and his family, and John Wilner and the wedding party from Cosmos; Delmar Holdgrafer, Gail Kloos, Marilynn Stallman, and Howard Hennen from Donnelly; Kathy Petron from Effie; Tracy and Marvin Christensen, and Philip Chicos from Freeborn; Brenda Skime, Carol Peterson, Ken Bjerknes, and the press box crew from Gonvick; Mary Trandem from Halstad; Brett Larson; and Sue Lyback-Dahl from Isle; Curt Johnson and the Jasper Stone Company crew from Jasper; Raymer and Louise Hoyum, and Millie Miller from Kelliher; Dave DeLost from Longville; Jerome and Nancy Haggenmiller, the folks at Olstad's Resort, and Deanna Schultz from Miltona; Gerhardt and Esther Schmidt, Helyna Mack, Fritz Fraelich, and Glen Hopp from Nicollet; LeRoy Strei, Cliff Olson, Emil Van Erem, and Don Teske from Odessa; Larry Ladd, Ralph Fowlds, and Terry Kullhem from Palisade; Linda and Dean Oquist from Quamba; Gene Knutson from Roosevelt; Bob Grams, and George Parrish from Storden; Duane and Marian Sarbaum, and the Corner Cafe gang from Taunton; Father Greg Mastey and Dan Hovland from Upsala; Dean Haarstick, Ron Goodman, and Roger Hanson from Vergas; Rosemary Jankowski and Bear MacCoy from Winton, Suzanne and Toby Crossman, and Pete Solberg from Yucatan; and Ken Markham, Steve Kramer, and Cathryn Peters from Zumbro Falls. Also, special thanks to my parents Audrey and Roger Andersen, John Beulke, Shannon Brady, Lynn Strong-Riley and Pat Riley, Bill Holm and Marcy Brekken, Bob Firth, John Kolness, Ron and Sylvia Asp, Becca Strong, Mary Walker, Melinda Smith, Michael LaTour, Karen Moen, the gang at Ciatti's, and the thoughtful person who invented cruise control.

Designed by

Barbara Arney

Stillwater, MN

Typeface is

Novarese